Books

Frances Wilkins

Batsford Academic and Educational Ltd   London

Typeset by DP Press, Sevenoaks
and printed in Great Britain by
R.J. Acford,
Chichester, Sussex
for the publishers
Batsford Academic and Educational Ltd,
an imprint of B T Batsford Ltd,
4 Fitzhardinge Street
London W1H 0AH

ISBN 0 7134 4057 0

ACKNOWLEDGMENT

The Author and Publishers would like to
thank the following for their kind permission to reproduce copyright illustrations:
BBC Hulton Picture Library, figs 6, 7, 10,
14, 18, 20, 21, 22, 23, 24, 26, 27, 28,
30, 38, 40, 44, 47, 48, 54, 58, 60; The
Bodleian Library, fig 15; The Trustees of
the British Museum, figs 2, 11, 13; Camera
Press Ltd, fig 4; Mary Evans Picture Library,
figs 56, 59; Pat Hodgson Picture Library,
figs 1, 16, 25, 32, 41, 42, 46; Anthony F.
Kersting, fig 55; The Mansell Collection,
figs 3, 5, 8, 19, 33; The *Times*, fig 43; John
Topham Picture Library, figs 53, 57, 61;
Victoria and Albert Museum, fig 9. The
pictures were researched by Pat Hodgson.

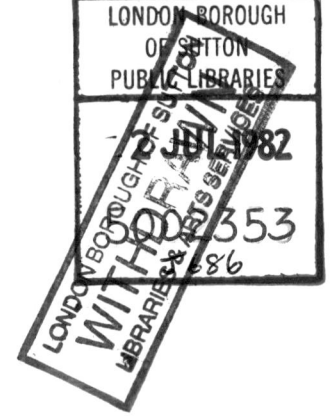

Contents

Acknowledgment   2

List of Illustrations   4

1   The First Books   5

2   Books Come to Britain   10

3   The Days Before Printing   16

4   The First Printed Books   22

5   The Spread of Printing   31

6   The Beginning of the Book Trade   36

7   Children's Books   41

8   Newspapers and Magazines   48

9   Books for Everyone   55

10 Libraries   62

Date List   69

Books for Further Reading   70

Index   71

List of
Illustrations

1 Egyptian hieroglyphics 5
2 Cuneiform writing 6
3 Egyptian scribes 7
4 Dead Sea scrolls 9
5 A monk illuminating 10
6 Lindisfarne Gospels 11
7 Lindisfarne Gospels 11
8 The Venerable Bede 12
9 The Book of Gospels 13
10 The Book of Kells 14
11 The Benedictional of St Aethelwold 15
12 Norman letter 17
13 The Luttrell Psalter 18
14 Jean Mielot 19
15 "The Romance of Alexander" 20
16 John Wyclif's Bible 21
17 Paper-making 22
18 Chinese printers 23
19 Johan Gutenberg 25
20 Movable type 26
21 Fust and Schoeffer's second Psalter 27
22 "The Recuyell of the Histories of Troy" 28
23 "The Canterbury Tales" 29
24 Caxton's advertisement 29
25 Colophons 32
26 Printer's workshop 32
27 Tyndale's New Testament 33
28 Chained Bible 34
29 Sidney's "Arcadia" 37
30 "Troilus and Cressida" 37
31 "Coryats Crudities" 39

32 "The Four Riders" 38
33 "The Dance of Death" 38
34 "The History of Solomon Serious" 42
35 Chapbook 43
36 Chapbook 43
37 "Jack the Giant Killer" 43
38 "Cinderella" 44
39 "Alice through the Looking Glass" 47
40 "Under the Window" 46
41 Children's book advertisements 47
42 "The Spectator" 49
43 "The Times" 50
44 "The Times" 50
45 "Tit-Bits" 52
46 "The Boy's Own Paper" 54
47 Hand printing press 56
48 Steam-powered printing machine 56
49 Linotype machine 57
50 Book binders 57
51 Leather bindings 58
52 The Bookseller 58
53 Penguins at Waterloo 59
54 "The Pickwick Papers" 60
55 The Bodleian Library 62
56 British Museum reading room 63
57 Circular Reading Room, British Library 64
58 Hall's Library, Margate 64
59 The Manchester Free Library 65
60 Camp-field Library, Manchester 66
61 A public library, 1950s 67

1
The First Books

The Ancient Egyptians called writing "the speech of the gods". They thought it was a magic means of communication, which only the priests could understand. They never guessed that one day almost everyone would learn to read and write, and that books would be a means of spreading so much information and pleasure.

The Egyptians first learnt to write six or seven thousand years ago, but, at first, they only used writing to commemorate some very important event. Their writing has been found, for instance, painted or carved on wood or stone in the tombs of some of the earliest pharaohs, or Ancient Egyptian kings.

1   Egyptian hieroglyphics painted on the walls of the tomb of Sen-Nufer, Valley of the Kings, Thebes.

This very early form of writing is known as hieroglyphic writing. It had no letters or alphabet; each hieroglyph (picture or symbol) represented a separate object or idea. A thin wavy line, for example, might mean the sea or a river, while a pair of horns meant a cow, and a bow and arrow a huntsman.

The Egyptians were not the only early people who could read and write. The Babylonians and the Assyrians, among others, developed a way of writing called "cuneiform", because of its shape. They wrote by pressing a kind of pen with a wedge-shaped end into tablets of soft clay, and these tablets were

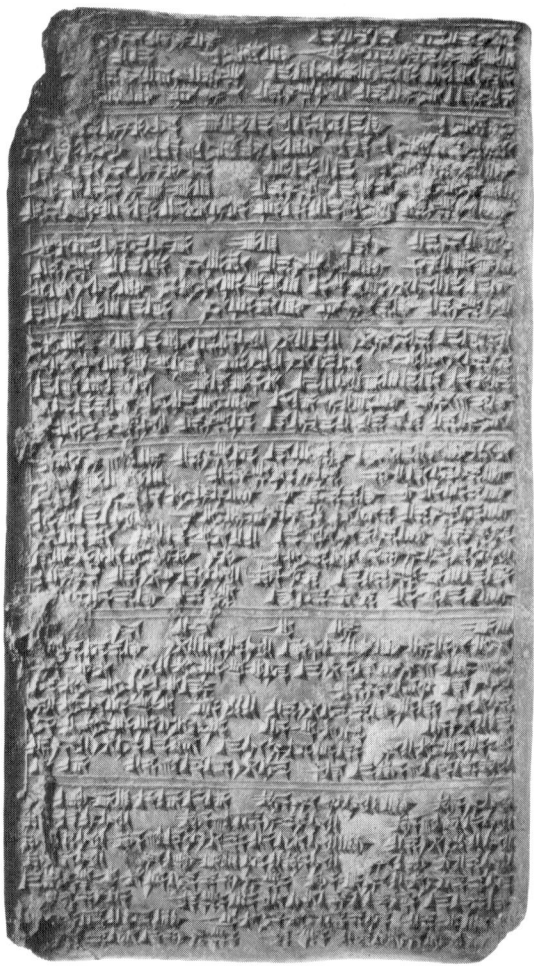

2 Cuneiform writing on a clay tablet from El Amarna.

then baked in an oven, or dried in the sun, until they were hard. Sometimes the tablets were even collected together to form a kind of book. They were numbered, just as we number our pages, and then all arranged together on a shelf. In a place called Sippar, in present-day Iraq, thousands of these clay tablets have been found, all carefully numbered and still in their correct places on the shelves, just as the scholars left them more than three thousand years ago.

But it was the Egyptians who made the next great advance. In the muddy swamps around the delta of the River Nile there grew a reed called papyrus. The stalk of this reed was sometimes as much as five metres tall, and as thick as a man's arm, and at the top there grew some fine, feathery foliage. The Egyptians cut the pith of this plant into short pieces. Then they split the pieces with a sharp knife into as many very thin strips as they could. They next laid the strips side by side on a flat surface, covered them with some kind of gum, and placed another layer of strips over them at right angles to the first. The strips were then pressed under some weights and finally dried in the sun. Then they were polished by rubbing them with a smooth piece of stone or a shell. The result was a sheet of rather tough paper, usually about 7 or 8 centimetres wide and about 16 or 17 centimetres long, on which people were able to write or draw.

Sheets of papyrus were often used singly for such things as letters or bills, but sometimes several of them were glued or sewn together to make a long scroll with a stick at one end. The longest known strip of papyrus is in the British Museum, in London. It is a chronicle of the reign of Pharaoh Rameses II, and it is nearly 44 metres long.

As time went on, not only writing materials but the art of writing itself began to change. After centuries of hieroglyphics and other kinds of picture writing, the Phoenicians invented the earliest alphabet. It had twenty-two letters, including some signs or letters that had been used by the Egyptians, but,

3 Egyptian scribes, about 1500 BC.

curiously enough, all the letters were consonants. The earliest known example of Phoenician writing is seen on what is called the Moabite Stone. This was found just over a hundred years ago on the shores of the Dead Sea. It was written in 890 BC, and describes a war between the King of Moab and the King of Israel, which is also related in the Bible (2 Kings chapter 3).

Later, the Ancient Greeks adopted the Phoenician alphabet. However, they found that they needed some vowels, so they changed some of the consonant signs into vowels and added a few other vowels of their own. Then in about the seventh century BC the Romans invented another alphabet, based loosely on the one the Greeks had invented. It is the Roman alphabet that we are still using in our country today.

From about the first century BC onwards the Romans also became interested in books. (They were not, of course, like the books we have today, but long papyrus rolls.) One of the first successful publishers was a wealthy author and scholar named Titus Atticus (109–32 BC), who published the works of the great Roman orator Cicero. Like all publishers in Ancient Rome, Titus Atticus used slaves to copy out his books. One of the slaves would read the original manuscript aloud while a number of other slaves would all busily write it down. Naturally, mistakes of one kind or another could very easily creep into books produced like this, but the books of Titus Atticus were renowned for their quality and accuracy.

Papyrus rolls had many disadvantages. They had no index or page numbers, and they had to be held at each end all the time they were being read. Nevertheless, it was not until early Christian times that a different way of making a book, by folding pieces of paper and stitching them together, as we do today, was invented.

This new type of book was called a codex (the plural is codices). No one knows exactly when or where codices were first invented, but they were certainly known by the beginning of the second century AD. Some of the most famous codices are copies of parts of the Bible. One of the oldest is the Codex Sinaiticus, which was written in the fourth century AD. It was discovered on Mount Sinai, in Egypt, in 1844, and can now be seen in the British Museum, in London.

These old codices were all written on sheets of papyrus. In a hot, dry country like Egypt papyrus lasted extremely well. In fact, as well as the codices, an enormous number of Egyptian papyrus rolls have been found, in almost perfect condition, with their ink apparently just as black as the day they were written. But papyrus rots as soon as it gets damp, so it was a great step forward when people discovered yet another material on which they could write.

The story goes that in the second century BC the King of Pergamon, in Asia Minor, asked a pharaoh called Ptolemy to send him some papyrus so that he could form a great library. Ptolemy did not trust the King of Pergamon, however, so he refused. This meant that the King of Pergamon had to think of another material on which people could write. His idea was to use the skin of cows, sheep and goats, and when thoroughly cleaned and smoothed with pumice stone, it did indeed make an excellent writing surface. It is called parchment.

Papyrus was normally so cheap and plentiful, however, that it was not until about the fourth century AD that parchment finally took its place for all ordinary, everyday purposes. For more important documents, it was generally replaced by vellum (the skin of very young animals), which was so smooth and flexible that it was by far the best writing surface that has ever been discovered.

About the same time as parchment and vellum finally replaced papyrus as the materials on which to write, the codex also became recognized as far superior to the scroll. So scribes everywhere were soon busy with the enormous task of rewriting all the great literature of the past on either parchment or vellum in the new codex form.

One of the very first books to be written in codex form was the Bible. The Emperor Constantine, the first Christian ruler of the Roman Empire, ordered fifty copies in Greek to be written as codices on vellum. He had just moved the capital of his great empire from Rome to Constantinople (now called Istanbul), and he wanted the Bibles for a great new library that he had decided to found there.

An important change that occurred when the codices on parchment or vellum replaced the old papyrus rolls was that illustrations at once began to be quite commonplace. In the Vatican Library, in Rome, there is a fourth-century codex version of the poems of Virgil with nearly fifty coloured pictures, and in Milan there is a fragment of the Iliad of much the same date which has fifty-eight.

4   A fragment of the Dead Sea scrolls. These Hebrew and Aramaic writings of parts of the Old Testament, dating from about 135 BC–70 AD, were first found in 1947, in an area north of the Dead Sea.

2
Books Come to Britain

"Every brother is to have a book given to him from the monastery library at the beginning of Lent, and by the end of Lent he should have finished reading it." These are the words of St Benedict, the founder of one of the earliest Christian monasteries, at a place called Monte Cassino, in Italy, in 528 AD. Monks must never be idle, said St Benedict, because

5   A monk illuminating, about 1200.

idleness is the enemy of the soul. So, whenever a monk had a few moments to spare, he was either to pray or to read a book. The monks also had special reading hours when they had to occupy themselves with a book, and they had to listen to someone reading to them while they were having their meals.

Similar rules were made in all the other monasteries of the time, and this meant that every monastery had to have its own library where the monks could obtain the books they had to read. Therefore, in every monastery there were a certain number of monks who spent virtually all their time, except when they were at prayer, making new copies of books which could be added to their library.

The monks wrote the books in a special room called the scriptorium. They always sat by a window, and never worked after dark in case a candle should fall over and set light to their work. No one in the scriptorium was ever allowed to speak. The monks had a special sign language, which they used so that they would not disturb each other.

The desk at which a monk sat was always steeply sloping. Beside the desk he had a small cupboard in which he could put all his tools. These included pens, which were made from goose quills, several pots of inks and colours, and a knife to cut his quills into shape and to scratch out any mistakes he made on the parchment.

The monks not only cut their own quills, but also made their own inks. One shade of blue was made from a stone called lapis lazuli and one shade of green was made from verdigris. Most of the other colours were made from various berries and barks, and were often very skilfully mixed together by the monks to produce beautiful shades. The gold that was often used to decorate the books was always real gold, however. It was sometimes ground into a powder and mixed with white of egg to make a fine paint. Alternatively, it was beaten out until it became as thin as tissue paper, and then stuck on to the page with a special kind of glue.

A monk always began by writing all the words that had to appear in black. Then he handed the book over to the rubricator, who added any notes that were needed in the margin in red. Finally, if the book was to be illustrated, as it usually was, it would be passed to yet another monk, who would add beautiful pictures in all the spaces that had been specially left for them.

Some of the favourite subjects for illustrations were strange, mythical animals, but the monks also drew all the interesting plants and animals which they saw in the woods and fields. Some of the pictures were miniatures, about 5–7 centimetres square, while others were full-page illustrations, usually surrounded by wide borders of flowers and leaves. The colours which the monks liked most were bright reds and blues, but they also liked shining gold, and small amounts of green, yellow and purple. So it is hardly surprising that the books are said to have been "illuminated" or "lit up", as the pictures often seem to glow with a special light of their own.

Once the writing and illustrations were all finished, the pages would be stitched together. Then the same thread used for stitching the pages would be put through the wooden

6 An illuminated letter at the beginning of St Matthew's Gospel, in the Lindisfarne Gospels.

7 An illustration of St Matthew, from the Lindisfarne Gospels.

boards that formed the front and back covers. These boards were then covered with leather with beautifully coloured designs on it, or even with sheets of silver and gold encrusted with precious stones. Other books had wooden covers, often carved with scenes from the Bible. The wood was usually beech, and it is from the German word for beech ("buch") that we get our English word "book". All these books were kept in strong wooden chests, with solid locks, as they were naturally very valuable having taken so long to make.

Some of the finest manuscripts at this period were produced in the north of England. One of the most famous of all is the Lindisfarne Gospels, which dates from about 698 AD. It was probably written and illustrated by Eadfrith, who at that time was the Bishop of Lindisfarne, a tiny island not far from Berwick-upon-Tweed, in Northumbria.

The Lindisfarne manuscript was nearly lost some two hundred years after it was written. Apparently, one of the monks dropped it into the sea while they were fleeing from hordes of marauding Danes. It is said to have been found again at low tide, however, by the help of a miracle, which made the sea go out nearly five kilometres from the shore. The Lindisfarne manuscript is now in the British Museum. It contains the four gospels in Latin, with a full-page portrait of each of the four evangelists. Although the marks left by the water can still be seen on the book, it is, on the whole, in excellent condition, bearing in mind its great age.

The best-known writer in these early times was the Venerable Bede. He was born in Durham in about 673 AD and studied at a monastery there before joining another religious community at Jarrow. Bede wrote books in Latin about the saints and about the Bible. He also wrote books on grammar and history, as well as a certain number of hymns. His most famous book, however, is his "Ecclesiastical History of England", which tells us practically all we know about England at that period. Bede also translated St John's

Gospel from Latin into Anglo-Saxon. He is said to have died just as he had dictated the very last words to a young scribe.

The earliest Anglo-Saxon poet of whom we know also lived in the north of England. His name was Caedmon, and he was a cowherd at a monastery at Whitby, in Yorkshire, towards the end of the seventh century. One night he is said to have had a dream that he must sing about the creation of the world, and although he had no learning and had never sung before, he made up and sang some of the very first English poetry.

8   The Venerable Bede, portrayed in a book called "Lives of the Saints" by Baring-Gould, 1897.

12

9   A beautifully ornamented cover for The Book of Gospels.

10 A page from the Book of Kells.

One of the most beautiful of all the early books was produced in Ireland. It is a wonderful illuminated manuscript which has come to be known as the Book of Kells. It was probably written in the monastery of Kells, in County Antrim, in about 800 AD, and is now in the library of Trinity College in Dublin. The Book of Kells consists of the first four books of the New Testament. The text is superbly written in a fine, regular hand, and is beautifully decorated with little designs in colour. There are also such exquisite illustrations of plants and animals, as well as drawings of characters from the Bible, that people used to say that they must have been drawn by angels.

Another remarkable work that belongs to this period is the long epic poem "Beowulf". It was probably made up in about 700 AD, but the oldest surviving written copy (now in the British Museum) dates from about the year 1000. Although the story is written in English, it has nothing to do with this country, but retells a Scandinavian legend about a monster called Grendel who was overcome by a young warrior named Beowulf and his companions.

King Alfred the Great (849–901) also did a great deal for English literature. There is a story that as a boy he was given a beautiful book by his mother because he was the first of her children to learn to read. Whether this is true or not, when he grew up he certainly translated quite a number of books

11 A page from the Benedictional of
St Aethelwold, showing St Etheldreda, abbess of
Ely, who died in AD 679.

(including Bede's "Ecclesiastical History") from Latin into English. He also wrote the earlier part of our first English history book, the "Anglo-Saxon Chronicle", which was continued after his death and finally completed in 1154.

There are a number of other very early books that can still be seen in museums. In the library of Lichfield Cathedral, in Staffordshire, for instance, there is a very old manuscript called the Gospels of St Chad. There is another ancient copy of the Gospels in the Bodleian Library at Oxford, and yet another in Lambeth Palace, the London home of the Archbishop of Canterbury. Perhaps the most interesting book of all, however, comes from Winchester and is now in the British Museum. It is called the Benedictional of St Aethelwold, and contains the blessings to be used by the bishop at various times of the year. It has thirty full-page illustrations, as well as many other richly decorated pages, and it ends with the request that anyone who reads it will say a prayer for "Godeman, the writer".

3
The Days Before Printing

One of the greatest treasures that still remains from Norman times is the Domesday Book. It was compiled in 1087, in the face of great popular resentment, by order of William the Conqueror. William wanted to know how many people lived in each town or village, what land they owned and what work they did, and he knew that the only way to find out was to make a complete survey of the country. The book did not actually cover the whole of England, however. Northumbria, Cumbria and northern Lancashire were omitted, and three other counties (Essex, Suffolk and Norfolk) were included in a smaller, separate volume. Nevertheless, the Domesday Book (which was written in Latin) is still a unique record of the period, unequalled in any other country or any other century.

The Domesday Book is now on display at the Public Record Office Museum, in London. It is still kept in the chest which was made to contain it, and is in remarkably good condition for its age. Oddly enough, though, the name "Domesday Book", which means "a record from which there is no appeal", was only given to the book about sixty or seventy years after it was written.

Once the Normans had conquered Britain, they wanted everyone to be Christian, and so they decided to build a great many new monasteries all over the country. Many of them were much larger and more important than the monasteries of Saxon times, but the main occupation of the monks was still to copy out the Bible and the missal, as the Roman Catholic prayer book is called.

In some of the monasteries the monks still wrote in a scriptorium, but in others each monk had his own small cell (or carral) by the side of the cloisters. Each of these little cells was only about a metre or two square, and merely contained a desk and stool, and perhaps a small cupboard for manuscripts.

By the end of the thirteenth century the monks were not only copying out the Bible and the missal. They were often making copies of the psalter, which is the old name for a book of psalms, as well. At this period, though, a psalter contained a great deal more than just the psalms, and was really a kind of general reference book for the monks. The first part of the psalter was always a calendar of the Church's year. It showed all the saints' days and festivals of the Church, written in red. (This is the reason why we still call an important or exciting day a "red letter day".) Then there were several pages of pictures, usually scenes from the life of Christ. After this came the first page of the psalms themselves. It was generally the most beautiful and elaborate page in the whole book. Finally came the rest of the psalms, divided into sections for each day, and usually with a richly ornamented page at the beginning of each section.

12 This letter from an early twelfth-century book shows the Norman style of illumination. Laymen listen to the prophet.

The most famous psalter still in existence is known as the Luttrell Psalter. It was probably written in about 1340, and is now in the British Museum, in London. It shows almost every aspect of everyday life at this period, from a doctor examining a patient to women preparing and cooking food for their families.

Another book which became famous in the late thirteenth century was called the Golden Legend. It was written by a Dominican monk named de Voragine, who lived in Genoa, in Italy. It described the lives of the saints and all the miracles they had performed, and monks in nearly every monastery in Europe were kept busy copying it out.

By the fifteenth century psalters were becoming less and less popular, but there was an ever increasing demand for missals, as more and more people knew how to read. Quite a large number of these missals are still in existence, including a very beautiful and interesting one which was made for Sherborne Abbey, in Dorset. We even know the name of the monk who copied out this book, because it says several times, "John Whas, a monk, laboured at writing this book". We also know that the artist was called John Siferwas, because he painted a picture of himself on one page of the missal, with his name underneath it.

As well as a missal for public worship, a wealthy person often had another book for private worship. This was called a Book of Hours, because it contained prayers which were to be said at various hours of the day. These books were usually only pocket-size, but they had wonderful illustrations, and were generally full of lavish decorations, as well.

17

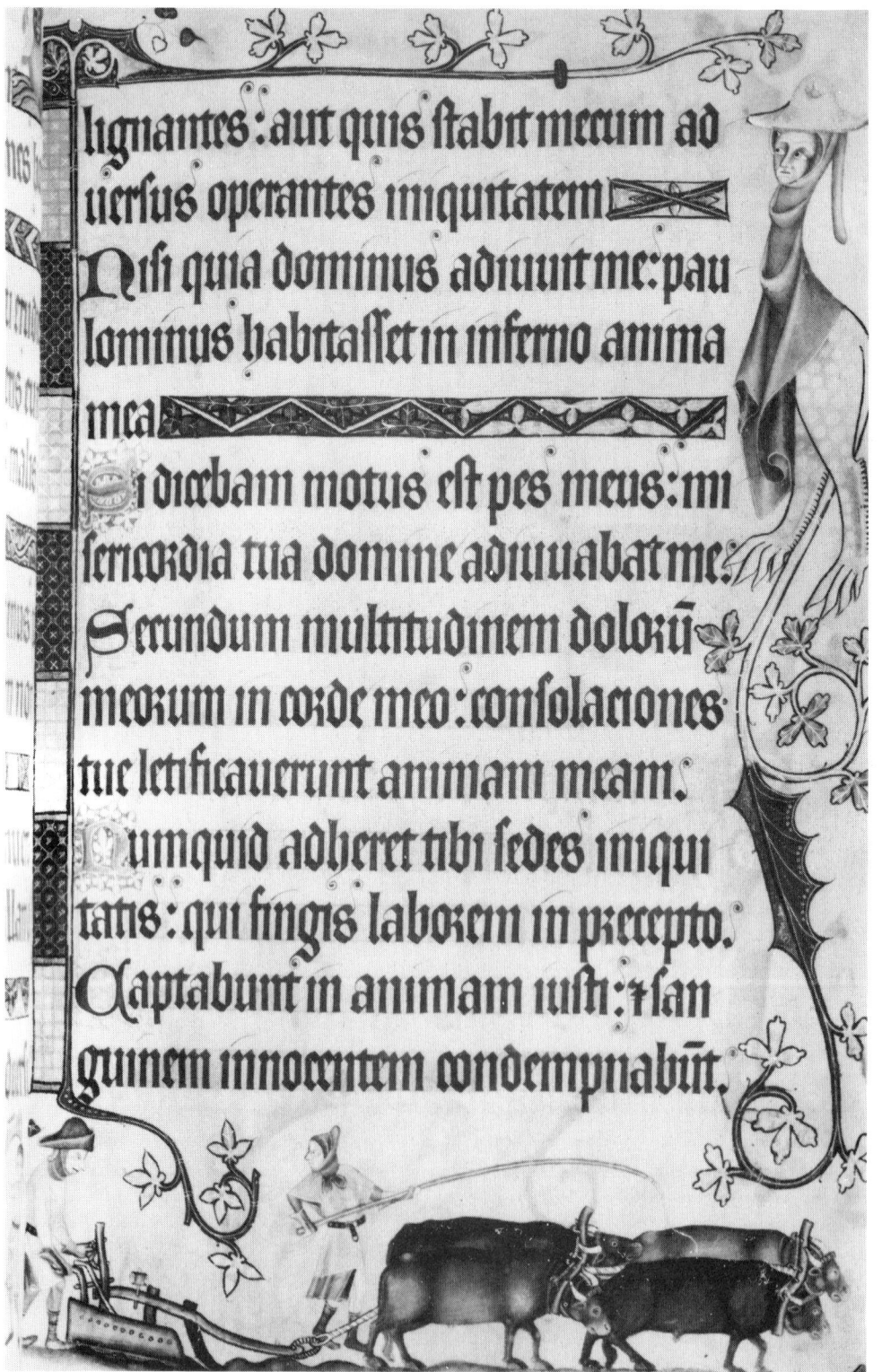

lignantes : aut quis stabit mecum ad
uersus operantes iniquitatem

Nisi quia dominus adiuuit me : pau
lominus habitasset in inferno anima
mea

Si dicebam motus est pes meus : mi
sericordia tua domine adiuuabat me.

Secundum multitudinem doloru
meorum in corde meo : consolaciones
tue letificauerunt animam meam.

Numquid adheret tibi sedes iniqui
tatis : qui fingis laborem in precepto.

Captabunt in animam iusti : 7 san
guinem innocentem condempnabut.

13 A page from the Luttrell Psalter.

14 A portrait of Jean Mielot, Secretary to Philip the Good, Duke of Burgundy. He is at work copying and illuminating books in an early library, c. 1430.

During the thirteenth and early fourteenth centuries many monks were kept busy copying out the Apocalypse. This is the last book in the Bible, sometimes known as the Book of Revelation. It contains far more imagery than any other book in the New Testament, and it gave the monks a wonderful opportunity to use their imagination and produce fantastic, colourful pictures. About forty copies of the Apocalypse from this period are still in existence. The most beautiful is in the library of Trinity College at Cambridge. It is a very large book, each folio measuring more than 40 by 30 centimetres, and it is believed to have been made for Eleanor of Provence, who was the wife of King Henry III.

By the twelfth or thirteenth century books were not only found in monasteries and churches. Many rich, noble families liked to own beautiful, illuminated manuscripts, and there were clerks (or scribes) in nearly all the great castles. Some very rich people even made small libraries for themselves, although they had to wait a very long time for the books while their clerks were copying them out.

Not all the books owned by these rich people were religious books. But at least until the end of the thirteenth century or even later all books set out to instruct. The idea of books which were written merely to entertain does not seem to have occurred to

19

people at this period.

A very popular history book, for instance, appeared in the middle of the twelfth century. It was written by a Welshman named Geoffrey of Monmouth, who later became the Bishop of St Asaph. Geoffrey claimed that his information came from some even earlier books, but it was probably just a collection of legends, such as the story of King Arthur and his Knights.

In the late thirteenth century a curious type of book called a bestiary became popular. At first glance it seemed to be a kind of natural history book, but in fact almost everything it contained was imaginary. It described dragons that breathed out flames, centaurs which were half man and half horse, and ant-lions, an incredible mixture of insect and lion. The aim of the book was not to teach people anything about animals. It was to try to make the readers understand the importance of correct Christian values and behaviour. For instance, in one book the reader is told that an elephant with a heavy load on its back is never able to rise to its feet without assistance, and that in the same way a man burdened with sin cannot rise without the help of Christ.

Nearly all books were written in Latin until the middle of the fourteenth century. Then a man named John Wyclif decided to write in English, the language that all the ordinary people could understand. In particular, he made the first translation of the Bible into English, and although it is not one of the versions still read today, it had a profound influence on the way English was spoken and written for many years afterwards.

Another of the very early writers in English was Geoffrey Chaucer. He was born in

15   Hare Shooting Men — an illustration from the margin of "The Romance of Alexander" written and illuminated in Flanders, c. 1340.

ye bigynnyng was ye word ꝫ ye word was
at god · ꝫ god was ye word yis was in ye bigy
nyng at god / alle yingis weren maad bihym:
and wyonten hym was maad no ping / yat mꝭ
yat was maad in hym was lyf · and ye lyf was
ye lyt of men / and lyt schyney in derknessis · and
derknessis comprenduden not it /

16   Part of John Wyclif's English Bible.

London about 1340, and as a boy became a page in the household of a rich nobleman. Later he became a soldier, then a courtier, then a customs officer and eventually Clerk of the Royal Works, in charge of repairs to all the royal palaces. Chaucer's most famous work, and his masterpiece, is "The Canterbury Tales". It is supposed to be a collection of stories told by a group of pilgrims on their way to visit the tomb of Thomas à Becket at Canterbury. The introduction or "prologue" is particularly famous, because it describes people of every type who lived at that period, the high and the low, the old and the young, the rogue and the honest citizen.

William Langland also wrote in English. He was born in a village in Shropshire, and spent all his early life among the poor country peasants. Later, when he was living in London, he wrote a great poem called "The Vision of Piers Plowman", in which he described in the form of dreams all the misery of the poor country people at that period.

4
The First Printed Books

Paper and Printing

Two very important discoveries had to be made before there were any books as we know them today. One was how to make paper, and the other was how to make a printing machine. Methods for doing both these things were invented in China in very

17 Paper can be made using old rags, as here in Scotland. The large stone wheel breaks up the rags.

early times, but they only arrived in Europe several centuries later.

Paper is said to have been made in China as early as 105 AD. No one has ever found any paper as old as that, but there are some pieces still in existence which were made before 137 AD. These, the oldest pieces of paper in the world, were found near a watchtower on the Great Wall of China, and are now in the British Museum, in London.

Paper was introduced into Spain by the Moors in the twelfth century, but it did not become popular immediately, because the Spaniards hated anything associated with the Moors, who had conquered their country. By 1270 the new invention had spread to Italy, and a few years later paper made in Italy was being imported fairly regularly into England.

Paper was usually made from old linen rags. These were soaked in water and beaten until they were reduced to a kind of runny pulp. The pulp was then diluted with more water, until it looked like a thick milk, and it was next poured into a tray with a flat bottom made of wire mesh, in order to drain. As the water gradually drained through the mesh, it left a sheet of matted fibres behind. This was put over a rope to dry, and once it was dry it became a sheet of coarse paper. There was always a crinkly edge to the paper, though, known as a deckle edge, caused by the water oozing out while the paper was in the tray, and this deckle edge is still a characteristic of hand-made paper today.

One advantage of paper over parchment was that it was much cheaper. It was only made of rags, instead of skins, and took much less time to prepare. But another great advantage of paper was that it was lighter and less cumbersome, and if it was made of good-quality materials it was almost as strong as parchment.

Printing was also invented in China, but not until the ninth century AD. This early printing was done by carving a whole page of writing (in reverse) onto a wooden block,

18   Chinese printers carve a page of writing.

法帖之圖也其鋪多設于琉璃廠
今名人字蹟刊於石上石上刷墨
以木錘用毡片旬而錘之取起則
也筆蹟絲毫不差今人臨之以學

23

then inking it and pressing it onto some paper. Later the Chinese learnt how to make movable type, which meant that each character (or letter) which went to make up the words could be printed separately and then used over and over again.

Johann Gutenberg

No one really knows who first used movable type in Europe. But it is generally thought to have been a German called Johann Gutenberg, who was born in Mainz in about the year 1400. No one knows, either, whether Gutenberg's first printing machine had type made of wood or of metal, but he was almost certainly using metal type before very long.

To make metal type Gutenberg first took some long pieces of wood, and carefully carved one letter of the alphabet in reverse on the end of each piece. Each stick was then pressed into a small square of clay, to leave a letter-shaped hollow, known as a matrix. Some pieces of wood were fitted round the matrix to form a narrow box, with the matrix at the bottom. Molten metal was then poured into the box and left to cool and harden. (Gutenberg discovered that the best metal to use was a mixture of lead, tin and antimony, the same metal that printers still use today.) Finally, the sides of the box were removed, and the metal was left in the shape of a long block with the letter standing out in reverse at one end.

Gutenberg probably started printing in Strasburg in about 1444. There are still three tiny fragments of three different books in existence which some people believe he printed there. One thing is certain, though, and that is that Gutenberg later returned to Mainz, where a wealthy goldsmith, named Johann Fust, lent him the money to set up another printing press.

The most important book printed by Gutenberg was the Gutenberg Bible. It first appeared in 1456, and is the earliest complete book printed in Europe with movable type.

Gutenberg probably made about three hundred copies of this Bible, and the forty which are still in existence today are among the most valuable books in the world.

Gutenberg never printed his name on any of his books. But in 1457 Johann Fust and a young man named Peter Schoeffer produced the first book that bore the name of the printers. It was a psalter, or book of psalms, and on the last page it says that the book was "fashioned by an ingenious invention of printing, without any driving of the pen", and then gives the printers' names.

There was another important innovation in this book, as well. None of the capital letters was filled in by hand by an illuminator or rubricator, as was the case in the books printed by Gutenberg. Instead, all the ornamental initials at the beginning of the various paragraphs and chapters were beautifully printed in three different colours.

William Caxton

The first English printer was William Caxton. He was born at Tenterden, in Kent, in about 1422, and when he was fifteen or sixteen years old he was apprenticed to a wool merchant in London. When his master died he went to Bruges, in Belgium, which was the centre of the wool trade in those days, and soon became a successful wool merchant himself. Caxton always had a great interest in books, however, and in his spare time he translated a book about the ancient city of Troy from French into English. So many people wanted to read this book that he decided he would set up his own small printing press, and print a few copies of it, as he had heard about the new art of printing while he was on a visit to Germany. This book must have been popular, because Caxton was soon printing a number of other books. We do not know the names of all of them, but one was a book about how to play chess. Then, after

19 Gutenberg is shown holding the letter A.

The true Effigies of Iohn Guttemberg Delineated from the Original Painting at Mentz in Germanie.

ABCDE
FGHIKLMNO
PQRSTVX
YZ

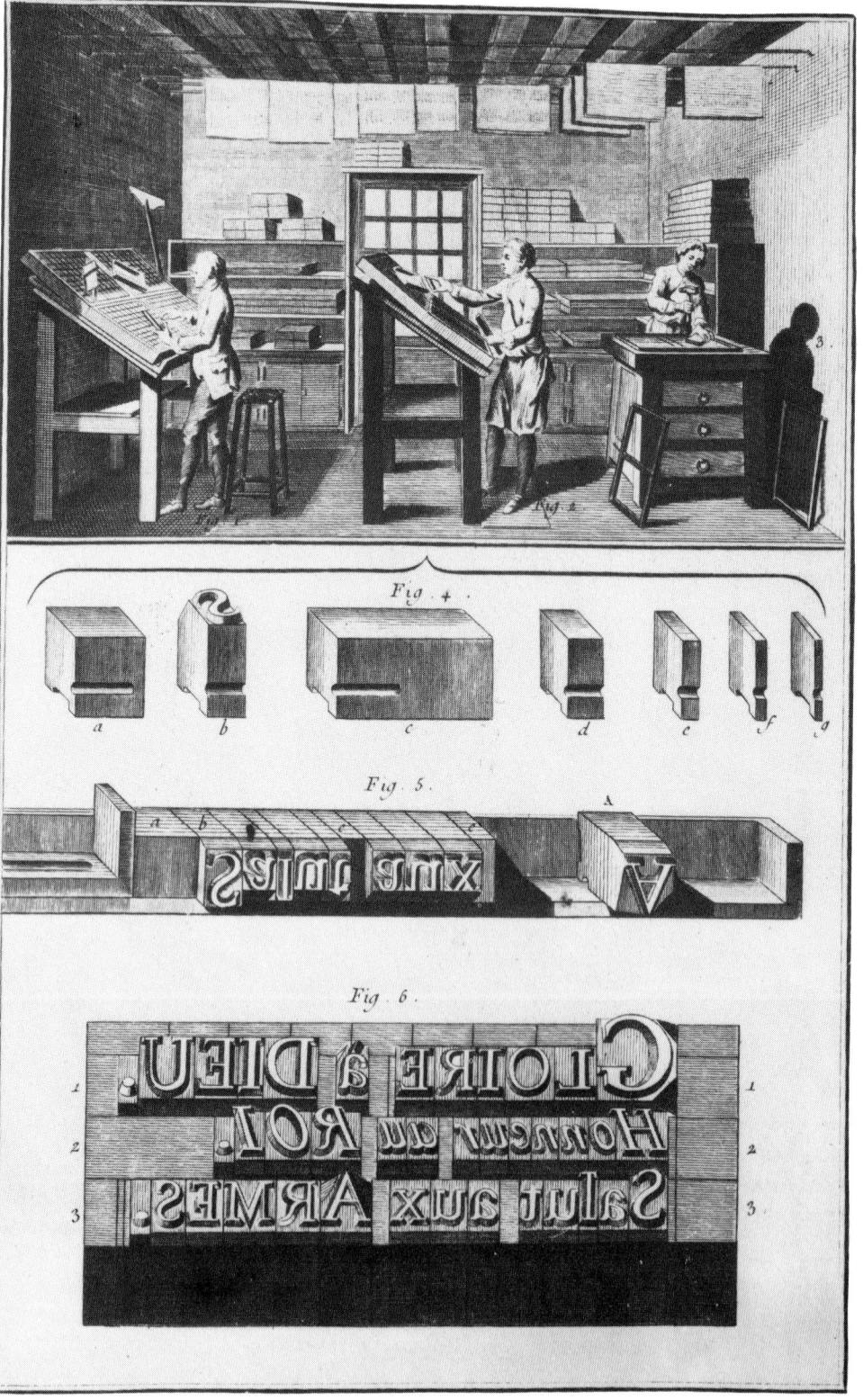

26

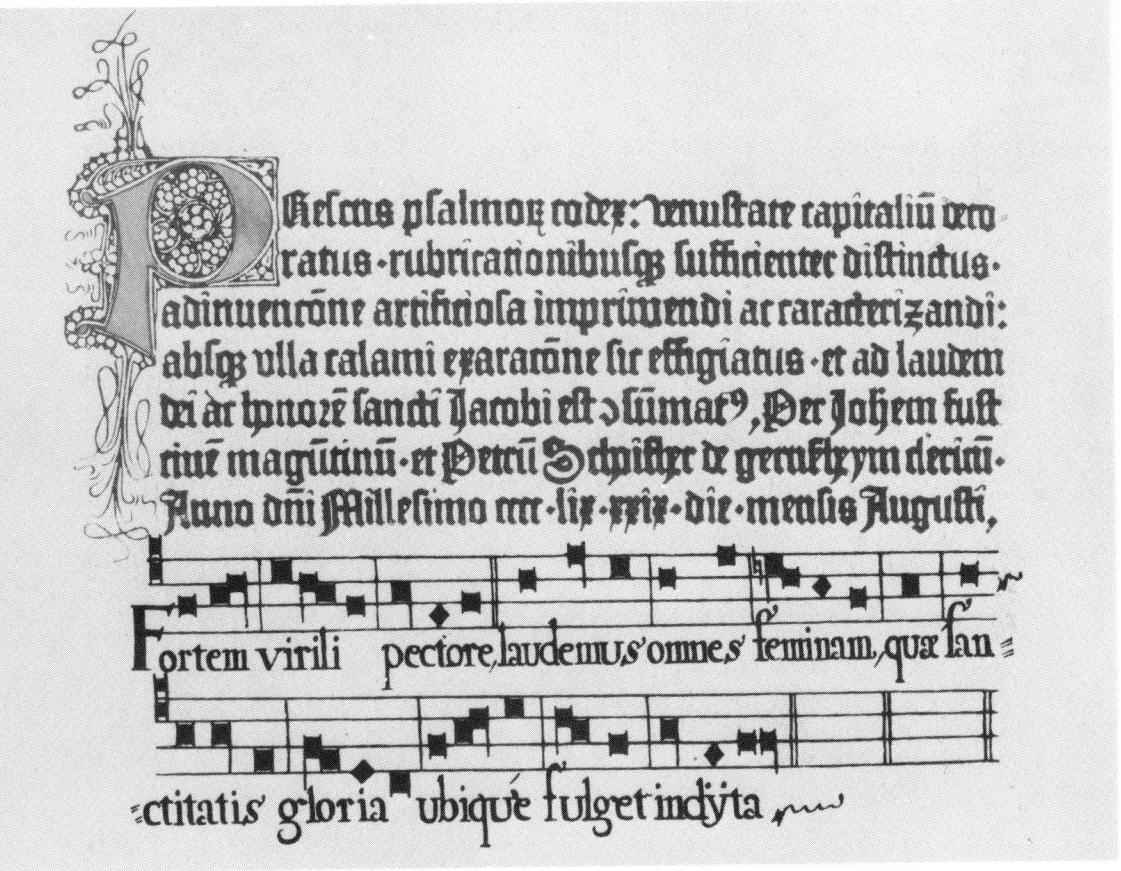

◀ 20 An illustration from Diderot's Encyclopedia in the eighteenth century shows how movable type was used.

21 Part of a page from Fust and Schoeffer's second Psalter, 1459.

being away from England for more than thirty years, Caxton at last decided to return home again and open a printing house here.

The place Caxton chose for his new printing house was near Westminster Abbey, in London. At that time the House of Commons met in the chapter-house of the Abbey, so Caxton may have thought that he could sell some books to the Members of Parliament. In any event, the sign outside his house was a white shield with a red vertical stripe or pale, so his address would have been "At the Sign of the Red Pale", London.

During the next fifteen years Caxton printed no fewer than ninety-six different books. The first, which appeared in 1477, was a small volume entitled "The Sayings of the Philosophers". Among the others he printed later were "The Canterbury Tales", "Morte d'Arthur" (an old romance about King Arthur and his knights) and "The Golden Legend", which was more than four hundred pages long. Caxton also printed the first book ever written in English for children. It appeared in 1477, and was called "The Book of Courtesy". It taught children how to behave, and among the many pieces of advice it gave was: "Do not dip your thumb in your drink, because it is not courteous".

Of course, all these early books took a very long time to print. When Caxton was printing "The Golden Legend", he wrote

Thus ende I this book whyche I haue translated aftir myn Auctor as nyghe as god hath gyuen me connyng to whom be gyuen the laude &
preysyng / And for as moche as in the wrytyng of the
same my penne is worn / myn hande wery & not stedfast
myn eyen dimed with ouermoche lokyng on the whit
paper / and my corage not so prone and redy to laboure
as hit hath ben / and that age crepeth on me dayly and
febleth all the bodye / and also be cause I haue promysid
to dyuerce gentilmen and to my frendes to addresse to hem
as hastely as I myght this sayd book / Therfore I haue
practysed & lerned at my grete charge and dispense to
ordeyne this said book in prynte aftir the maner & forme
as ye may here see and is not wreton with penne and
ynke as other bokes ben / to thende that euery man may
haue them attones / ffor all the bookes of this storye named the recule of the historyes of troyes thus enprynted
as ye here see were begonne in oon day / and also fynyss-
hid in oon day / whiche book I haue presented to my
sayd redoubtid lady as a fore is sayd. And she hath
well accepted hit / and largely rewarded me / wherfore
I beseche almyghty god to rewarde her euerlastyng blysse
aftir this lyf. Prayng her said grace and all them that
shall rede this book not to desdaigne the symple and rude
werke . nether to replye agaynst the sayyng of the ma-
tere touchyd in this book / thauwh hyt acorde not vn-
to the translacon of other whiche haue wreton hit / ffor
dyuerce men haue made dyuerce bookes / whiche in all
poyntes acorde not as Dictes . Dares . and Homerus
ffor dictes & homerus as grekes sayn and wryten favo-

22   A page from the first English printed book,
"The Recuyell (or collection) of the Histories of   Troy", printed by Caxton at Bruges, c. 1475.

23 A woodcut of the Friar from Chaucer's "Canterbury Tales", printed by Caxton in 1493.

24 Caxton's advertisement – the first English printed advertisement, c. 1477.

If it plese ony man spirituel or temporel to bye ony pyes of two and thre comemoraciõs of salisburi vse enpryntid after the forme of this preset lettre whiche ben wel and truly correct, late hym come to westmonester in to the almonesrye at the reed pale and he shal haue them good chepe ⸭

Suplico stet cedula

that it was taking so long that he was "half desperate to have accomplished it". The chief difficulty was that the printers never had enough letters to print a whole book, so they just put together the type for a few pages, printed these, and then had to rearrange the type for the next few pages.

Caxton sometimes advertised some of his books on small posters or handbills in the street. At the bottom of each poster he always added, in Latin, the words, "Please leave this handbill alone"! There seem to have been as many vandals and hooligans wandering around the towns looking for something to deface in Caxton's time as there are today!

Very early printed books were usually sold in loose sheets. Then the person who bought them could have them bound in any style or material he chose. In fact, it was not until the end of the sixteenth century that books were normally sold in leather bindings (often decorated with gold), and even later that cloth replaced leather.

Oddly enough, the early printers were not particularly proud of their work. In fact, even Gutenberg tried to make his books look as if they had been written by hand. The printers thought that people would think their books were so unattractive and dull that they often did not even include their names and the place and date of printing, and if they did they nearly always hid them away at the back of the book.

5
The Spread of Printing

In the Middle Ages nearly all craftsmen belonged to their own craft guild, an association of people who were all engaged in the same kind of craft or trade. One of these guilds was known as the Guild of Stationers, and its members were the craftsmen who supplied scribes with pens, parchment, book-binding materials and so on.

Once printing had been invented, the printers sometimes joined the Guild of Stationers, too. Whether Caxton himself was a member we do not know, but almost certainly some of his apprentices were. Caxton had quite a number of apprentices, and it was one of them, Wynkyn de Worde, who carried on the business at the "Sign of the Red Pale" after Caxton had died.

Some years later de Worde moved to a new house in Fleet Street. By this time Fleet Street was rapidly becoming the centre of the printing and bookselling trade in this country. It was also the place where large numbers of unbound books which had been printed abroad were stitched together, and then put into bindings and sold.

One of the most famous printers on the Continent was Aldus Manutius. He opened a printing house in Venice, in Italy, in about 1490. He was the first printer to produce small, cheap books that students were able to afford, and he once complained that he had so many customers that "there is scarcely time for me to blow my nose"! There are still many books printed by Manutius in various museums and collections. They can always be recognized by their colophon (or printer's mark) at the end. Every printer had his own colophon, and the one used by Manutius was an anchor (which stood for firmness or safety) with a dolphin (which stood for speed) twined around it.

Christopher Plantin, of Antwerp, in Belgium, was another famous printer. He printed books not only in French and Dutch, but also in Latin, Greek, German and English. He was also one of the first printers to put the title pages of his books at the front instead of at the back, so that as soon as the reader opened the book he saw its name and a list of contents.

Censorship

With the invention of printing, books became cheaper and much more plentiful, and they began to play an ever increasing part in the spreading of new ideas and opinions. Some of these ideas did not meet with the government's approval, however, usually either for religious or political reasons, and it was not long before the first censorship was set up. The first list of banned books in England was issued as early as 1529. It was drawn up for Henry VIII, who at that time was still a practising member of the Roman Catholic Church.

Richard Pynson, died 1530.

John Day, died 1584.

Wynkyn de Worde, flourished 1493—1533.

Robert Copland, died 1548.

Thomas Berthelet, died 1555.

Robert Wyer, flourished 1527—1542.

▲
25   The colophons of some early English printers.   **26**   A printer's workshop, c. 1600.
▼

The list included any books which were likely to spread the new religious ideas which were sweeping the whole of Europe at that time, or which were in any way likely to undermine the authority or teaching of the Church.

The book that caused the most controversy of all was the Bible. In earlier times if people had wanted to read the Bible in English they had always used Wyclif's version, which had been translated from the Latin. Then in about 1516 a man named William Tyndale began translating the New Testament into English from a Greek version that had been written by the great Dutch scholar, Erasmus. No one in England seemed very interested in Tyndale's new translation, though. Tyndale therefore went to Germany where Peter Schoeffer eventually printed three thousand copies of his work. The books reached England in 1526, but the Church immediately condemned them because they were translated from the Greek, and so differed in some ways from the Latin version that everyone was accustomed to reading.

Later a friend of Tyndale's, Miles Coverdale, printed the first complete Bible in English (the Old and New Testaments together). It was dedicated to Henry VIII, who had by then proclaimed himself the head of the Church of England. The King was so pleased with it that he gave orders in 1539 that a copy of it was to be placed in every parish church in the country for everyone to read. These Bibles were so large and heavy that special reading desks had to be set up to support them. Also they were usually attached to the desks with chains so that no one could take them away. These old chained Bibles can still be seen in a number of churches and cathedrals even today, including churches at York, Stratford-upon-Avon and Worcester.

Shortly afterwards, in 1542, the Guild of Stationers applied to the Crown for a charter. The Stationers did not want anyone to be allowed to practise the "art or mystery of printing" unless he was a member of the guild. In other words, they were asking for a "closed shop", but the government saw this as an

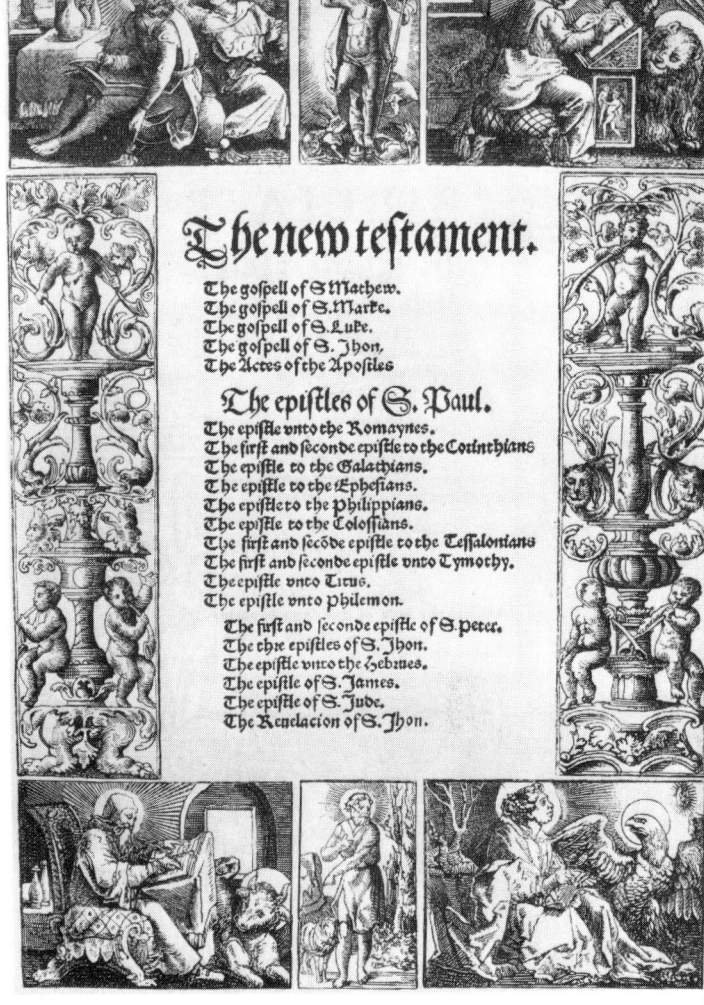

27   The title page of Tyndale's New Testament as published in 1536.

opportunity to keep even tighter control over the printers. In brief, the charter forbade the printing of anything unless it was licensed by the Crown. Also, no books on any subject (however innocuous) were allowed to be imported from abroad. This meant that the King and his ministers had complete control (at least in theory) over everything that was printed, or even read, in this country.

When James I came to the throne he even decided to revise the English version of the Bible. He asked fifty-four of the most eminent scholars of the day to undertake the work, and it took them four years. The Bible finally appeared in 1611, and was called the Authorised Version, as it was the version that was authorised to be read in all the churches

28   A chained Bible at St Paul's Cathedral, London.

from that time onwards.

Some printers were very angry, however, that they were not allowed to print what they wished. So some of them began printing books that had not been licensed and then put a false name and address at the back. Also books were often printed abroad (particularly in the Netherlands), and then smuggled into this country, and sold secretly to people who were known to be interested in them.

One man who was angered by this censorship was the poet John Milton. Indeed, he was so incensed that in 1644 he wrote a famous pamphlet on the subject called the "Areopagitica". This said: "It is as good almost to kill a man as a good book. Who kills a man kills a reasonable creature, but who destroys a good book kills reason itself."

Nevertheless, nearly twenty years later, in 1663, an Act was passed in Parliament that said that only twenty-one master printers were allowed to carry on their craft, and they were all in either London, Oxford or Cambridge. What was more, anything written about politics had to be passed by the Secretary of State before it was published, anything about the law by the Lord Chancellor, and most other books by either the Archbishop of Canterbury or the Bishop of London.

It was not until 1695, in fact, that the censorship was finally ended. By this time printing had been under the direct control of the Crown for nearly two hundred years. Once the censorship was removed, authors and editors were allowed to express any opinions

34

they pleased, even if these were critical of the Church or the government.

Newsbooks and News-sheets

When printing was first invented it was used exclusively for printing books. Day-to-day news, which today would appear in a newspaper, had to pass from person to person by word of mouth. No doubt these items were thought to be of such fleeting interest that it would hardly be worth all the slow, laborious effort that was needed to produce even a page of printing in those days.

In about 1513 little newsbooks began appearing from time to time, however. They were quite small (about 10 by 12 centimetres), and each edition contained a description of just one important event. One of these, called "True Encounter", gave an eye-witness account of the Battle of Flodden, and even had a front-page illustration (a woodcut) showing the battle in progress and the King with his crown in his hands.

Towards the end of the sixteenth century these newsbooks were appearing every few weeks. But they only appeared if the publishers thought there was some important news item to report. By this time there were also sheets carrying foreign news coming from other parts of Europe, particularly from Italy, and being distributed by some of the booksellers in London.

Each of these small newsbooks only dealt with one special subject. But in Venice, in Italy, there were news-sheets covering a wide range of topics as early as in 1566. These sheets were pasted up in the streets for anyone to read on payment of a small coin called a gazzetta, the word from which we get our popular present-day name for a paper, "The Gazette".

Oddly enough, the first paper in England which carried various items of news did not have a name. It was begun in about 1567 by John Wolfe, who had once been a printer's apprentice. Wolfe is sometimes called the "father of newspaper publishing", because he collected the contents of his paper from a wide range of different sources, just as newspaper editors do today.

6
The Beginning of the Book Trade

The early printers, like Caxton, produced their books almost entirely unaided. They often wrote, or at least translated, the manuscripts, cast the type and then printed, sewed and finally bound the books. They usually sold the books, as well, either on their own premises or perhaps at one of the great fairs which were held in all the larger towns in the Middle Ages.

As time went on, however, the book trade became more and more complicated. Some people decided to set themselves up as typefounders, some as printers, some as engravers and yet others as binders. In addition, there were the booksellers, who undertook to sell the books for the printers but did nothing themselves towards the actual production of the books.

Later there was another group of people, called the publishers. It was their job to buy books from the authors or printers and distribute them to the various booksellers. They did not pay the authors a great deal for their books, though, because in those days there was no copyright act, and once a book was published any other printer could copy it and sell it. In fact, a publisher usually just gave an author a small amount of money and a certain number of free copies of the book, which he could try to sell himself. For example, John Stow, who wrote "A Survey of London" in 1598, only received £3 and forty copies of his book from his publisher.

There was only one way a publisher could try to prevent people from copying a book. This was to enter the title with the Stationers' Company, which in theory gave him the sole right to publish this particular work. In very old books the words "Entered at Stationers' Hall" quite often appear on the first page, although even this does not always seem to have prevented unscrupulous printers from making their own copies and selling them.

Authors did not always rely entirely on their publishers for money, though. Sometimes a writer would put a very elaborate dedication in his book to some rich man who had agreed to be his patron. In return, the patron would give the author either a gift of money or a small pension, or he might even give him some post in his home, perhaps as a secretary or as a tutor to his children.

Popular Books

Despite all the difficulties, books poured from the presses during the sixteenth and seventeenth centuries. In fact, most people did not seem to care in the least about the quality of the printing as long as they had something to read. The reason for this was that from early Elizabethan times onwards more and more children were going to school, and discovering all the interest and information that there was to be found in a book.

29 The title page of Sir Philip Sidney's "Arcadia" shows that he wrote under the patronage of the Countess of Pembroke.

Among the books most in demand were the ancient classics. These were the works of the great Greek and Roman authors, either in their original tongues or translated into English. People also wanted to read the famous books written by English writers in earlier times, which they all knew by name, particularly the writings of Langland and Chaucer. The plays written by Shakespeare were also much in demand, although strangely enough his complete works were not printed until 1623, seven years after his death. When this "first folio", as it was called, was originally published, it cost £1, and it is now, more than three hundred years later, one of the most valuable books in the world.

30 The title page of Shakespeare's "Troilus and Cressida".

There was also a popular history book, called a "Chronicle", by Raphael Holinshed. It dealt with the history of Britain from the earliest times up to 1575, and was written in a clear, unadorned style. Its chief interest today, however, lies in the fact that Shakespeare used this book for practically all the information he needed when he was writing his historical plays.

There were several books on religion which were in great demand as well. Probably the most popular of all was a book usually known today as "The Book of Martyrs", by John Foxe. It described the persecution by the Catholics of all the people who were working for the Reformation during the reign of Mary Tudor, and tried to arouse as much anti-Catholic feeling as possible.

Some of the best-loved books at this period, however, were about travel and exploration. One of these describes the first complete circumnavigation of the globe by Sir Francis Drake in his ship "The Golden Hind". It was written by the ship's chaplain, Francis Fletcher, and printed by a man named Hakluyt, and even today it is still one of the most exciting and absorbing sea stories ever written.

It was the books of Sir Walter Raleigh which really caught people's imagination. First he wrote a stirring account of the last fight of his ship, the "Revenge", against almost overwhelming odds just off the Azores. Then in 1596 he published "The Discovery of the Large, Rich and Beautiful Empire of Guiana", which was full of detailed observations and quaint tales about this unknown corner of the world. But it was Raleigh's vast "History of the World from Creation to 130

31 The title page of a travel book by Thomas ▶
Coryat, 1611.

BC" that was his greatest triumph. It was written while he was imprisoned in the Tower of London, and published in 1614. Although Raleigh considered it to be unfinished, it was so highly regarded by the people of the time that it went into eleven editions in the following seventy-three years.

Illustrations

People knew how to print pictures, oddly enough, before they could print writing. But even in Caxton's time illustrations in this country were usually just simple outlines, without any real attempt at light and shade. The problem seems to have been that there were very few artists in England at that period skilful enough to make the very detailed woodblocks that were needed for really beautiful pictures. In fact, one woodblock

33 One of Holbein's drawings for "The Dance of Death". Compare this and figure 32 with the simple woodcut in figure 23.

32 A woodcut of "The Four Riders" by Albrecht Dürer, to illustrate the Apocalypse.

would sometimes be used for several illustrations in the same book. A view of a city, for instance, might represent London on one page, and Athens or even Jerusalem on another. In a book called "The Nuremberg Chronicle", published in Germany in 1493, there were no fewer than six hundred and forty-five separate pictures, but many of them were merely the same woodblocks used over and over again.

Books produced on the Continent at this period were sometimes illustrated by very famous artists. The great German artist, Albrecht Dürer, for example, made a series of drawings to illustrate the Apocalypse. Also a few years later (in 1538) Hans Holbein did fifty-eight exquisite drawings for a book called "The Dance of Death", which many people think are the finest woodcuts of the time still in existence.

As time went on, however, woodblocks gradually fell into disuse. Their place was taken by copperplate engravings, which were stronger and lasted much longer. People had known how to make copperplate engravings long before Caxton's time, but they had gone out of fashion in the early days of printing because, unlike woodblocks, they could not be printed at the same time as a sheet of type. To make a copperplate engraving the picture was first cut in the copper. Then the ink was poured into the sunken lines and the surface of the plate was wiped clean. A damp sheet of paper was then put over the plate, and the plate and the paper were pressed firmly together so that the ink was drawn out of the lines in the copper onto the paper.

Newspapers

Not only books, but also newspapers benefited from the rapid spread of printing. But rather oddly these early papers very rarely had any particular name, even if they were published every week. This may have been to protect the publishers, for they were turbulent times, and there was always the danger of expressing an opinion which was not in line with the ideas of the government. Then, just as people were becoming accustomed to having a newspaper, the papers ceased completely. Because of the political situation, no newspapers were officially allowed to be printed for six years, beginning in 1632. Nevertheless, there were a number of printers who defied the ban, and continued to produce news-sheets even at the risk of being sent to prison or transported for life.

During the Civil War, however, the situation suddenly improved. Both the Royalists and the Puritans wanted everyone to know their views, and papers began to appear in much the form in which we know them today. They had definite titles, were much taller and wider than books, appeared on regular days and were both dated and numbered, but (unlike today) they were always priced at one penny. All the newspaper owners naturally felt that they had to take sides politically. One of the two leading papers supported the King and its main rival supported the Puritans. Then, once the war was over, nearly all the old restrictions returned, and the two hundred or so newspapers that had flourished briefly during the fighting were reduced quickly to two.

It is interesting to note that already at this period newspapers included advertisements. These cost 6d (2½p) for each insertion, and must have helped to keep down the price of the papers. One early advertisement said: "If anyone who can draw Japan Figures well wants employment, or any boy whose genius lies that way wants to be an apprentice, if they will come to me I believe I can help them."

7
Children's Books

From the very beginning children's books have virtually always been written by adults. What is more, until quite recently they were almost invariably purchased for the children by adults as well. As a result, children's books remained, almost until the beginning of this century, what grown-ups thought that children ought to read rather than what the children themselves might have enjoyed.

As early as the sixteenth century a few books were already being published for children, but they were nearly all educational books of some kind, and were all meant to be used in schools. For example, a man named Roger Ascham, who was a famous classical scholar and tutor to Queen Elizabeth I when she was a child, wrote the first Latin grammar which was meant to be specially for children.

If children wanted to read story books in those days they had to read books for adults. But some of the books were quite interesting and entertaining, and have actually become favourites with many children today. They included stories about King Arthur and his Knights of the Round Table, tales about an adventurous knight called Guy of Warwick, and also Aesop's Fables, which were not originally written for children.

Books were still comparatively rare and highly prized at this period, however, so any child who was lucky enough to possess a book would have had to look after it very carefully. In fact, there is a copy of Aesop's Fables in the British Museum, published in 1585, which has written inside the cover: "James Dodson is my name and with my pen I write the same", then the date, 1690, more than one hundred years after the book had been printed.

The first story books written for children appeared in about 1650. But they were practically all written by Puritans, and their aim was to make the children think about their duty and about sin. One of them, by a writer named James Janeway, even asked the children if they had "ever shed a tear" when reading the book because it made them think of some of the wicked things they had done.

No books for children had pictures in them until the mid-seventeenth century. Then a few little A B C books appeared with a picture about 3 centimetres square above each letter. Also at about the same time the first book with illustrations for older children was published. It was called "The Visible World", and had a number of little woodcuts with descriptions underneath them in both English and Latin.

By the eighteenth century there was another kind of book that children often read, called a chapbook. These were little books of rhymes or stories which were sold from door to door by chapmen, or pedlars. The average chapbook was only about 10 by 5 centimetres, it had just a rough paper cover

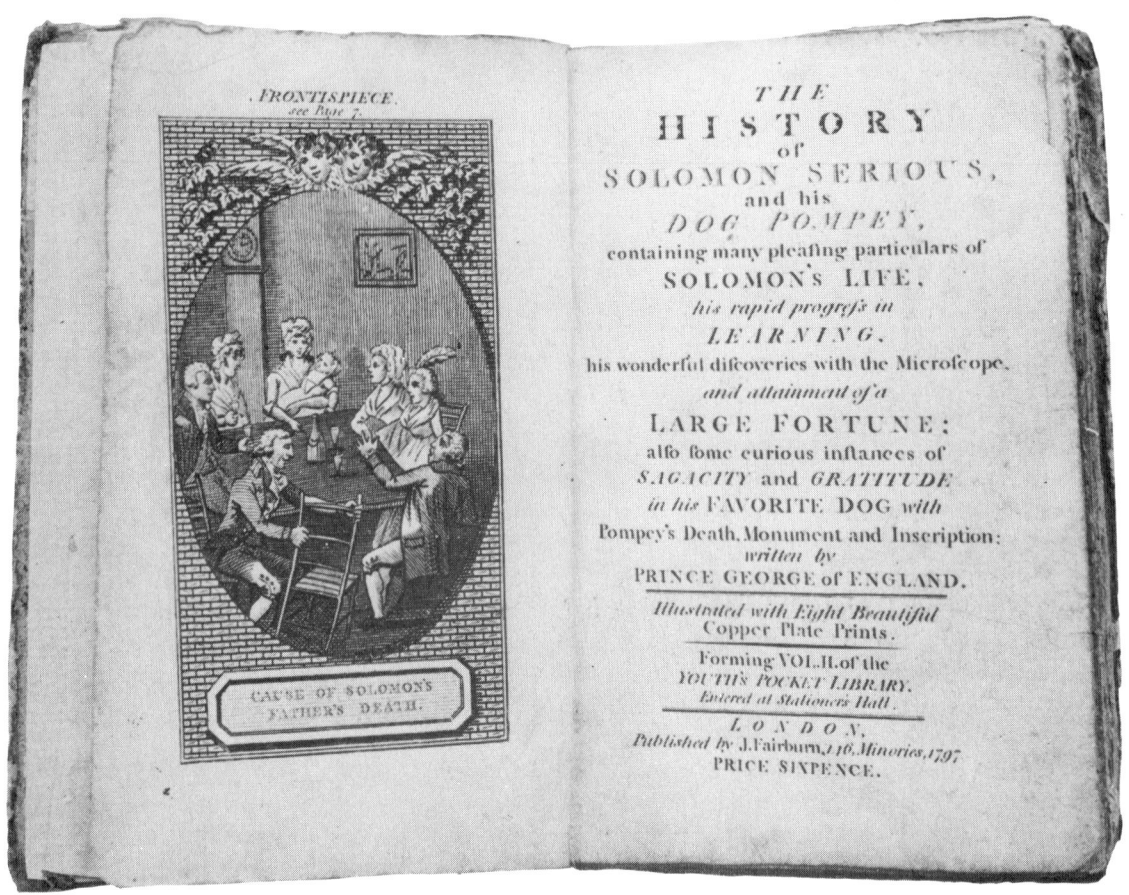

FRONTISPIECE.
see Plate 7.

CAUSE OF SOLOMON'S
FATHER'S DEATH.

THE
HISTORY
of
SOLOMON SERIOUS,
and his
DOG POMPEY,
containing many pleasing particulars of
SOLOMON's LIFE,
his rapid progress in
LEARNING,
his wonderful discoveries with the Microscope,
and attainment of a
LARGE FORTUNE:
also some curious instances of
SAGACITY and GRATITUDE
in his FAVORITE DOG with
Pompey's Death, Monument and Inscription:
written by
PRINCE GEORGE of ENGLAND.
Illustrated with Eight Beautiful
Copper Plate Prints.
Forming VOL. II. of the
YOUTH's POCKET LIBRARY.
Entered at Stationers Hall.
LONDON,
Published by J. Fairburn, 146, Minories, 1797.
PRICE SIXPENCE.

34 Moral education in an entertaining form, by Prince George of England.

(or even no cover at all), and the woodcuts that illustrated it were generally so clumsily printed that it was often quite difficult to make out what they showed. Nevertheless, the chapbooks cost only one, or perhaps two, pennies, and so they gave the less well-off children the first opportunity they had often had to own a book of their own. Some of the older children probably also read the chapbooks that were intended for the grown-ups, as they were full of old folk tales and fairy stories that had been handed down for generations.

It was not until 1744, however, that the first book appeared which was meant to amuse children as well as instruct them. This was called "A Little Pretty Pocket Book",

and was published by John Newbery at St Paul's Churchyard, in London. It was full of pictures of children flying kites, playing at hopscotch and blind-man's-buff, and even cricket (although it was being played with a curved bat and only two stumps), as well as verses to help the children learn the alphabet. The "Pocket Book" cost 6d, but if a ball and a pincushion were bought at the same time then the total cost for all three was 8d. The ball was presumably just to amuse the children, but the pincushion was obviously designed to try to win the approval of the grown-ups. One side of the pincushion was red and the other black, and a letter from "Jack the Giant Killer", which came with it, told the children to stick a pin in the red side whenever they did a good deed and a pin in the black side whenever they did a naughty one.

Quite a number of story books for child-

This book set forth at large for the
benefit of those
Who from being quite destitute, friend-
less and poor,
Would have a fine House, and a Coach
at the door.

U Up-and-Down, u

Here some go up and some go down,
To take their pastime at the fair ;
Just so it is the world all round,
Each has his pleasure, each his care.

35 and 36 Pages from two simple chapbooks published in York in about 1820 — one from "The House That Jack Built", another from an alphabet book.

ren began to appear in the second half of the eighteenth century. But, like the "Pocket Book", they were never written merely to amuse, but always to point a moral at the same time. Qualities like greed, selfishness and cruelty and, in particular, bad temper were always shown to lead to misery in the end, while their opposites, of course, led to

happiness. At least two of the books from this period were so exciting, however, that children still read them today. One was "Sandford and Merton", by Thomas Day,

37 A much more elaborate folding frontispiece to a colour fairy-tale booklet of the "penny plain and twopence coloured" period.

CINDERELLA

AND

THE GLASS SLIPPER.

and the other "The Fairchild Family", by Mrs Sherwood. Even the duller books were often made quite interesting by this period with delightful woodcuts, showing scenes from country life, animals, birds, farmyard scenes, shepherds and so on.

It was not until the end of the eighteenth century that the first children's books appeared which did not try to teach the children anything. These were books that retold the old fairy tales that had been handed down for centuries. There were also some new fairy stories, like "Cinderella", by a French writer called Perrault, although the slipper in the story, which was made of calfskin ("*veau*" in French) was carelessly translated into English as a slipper made of glass ("*verre*").

By this period even the poorest children wanted to have books of their own, but they often could not read very well, and so their books had to have as many pictures as possible. In some of the books the pictures were just black and white, but in others they were coloured, and this is the origin of the old phrase "a penny plain and twopence coloured". All the pictures were, in fact, just printed in black and white. But then some of the books were given to girls, aged about thirteen or fourteen, to colour, either at home or in a factory. One girl would put the green paint on all the trees, another the blue on all the skies, and yet another the pink on all the people's faces, and so on.

By the nineteenth century children's books were beginning to pour from the presses. Some were not only interesting and amusing, but beautifully printed and illustrated as well. Among them there were books of comic verses and riddles, and books of games of all kinds, but the majority were still serious books that usually set out to teach a moral. One of the most popular books of all contained the fairy stories written by the Grimm brothers. The first English edition appeared in 1823, amusingly illustrated by the cartoonist George Cruikshank. Then, in 1839,

came "Holiday House", by Catherine Sinclair, which was very popular at the time, followed in 1846 by the "Book of Nonsense", by Edward Lear.

Not long afterwards the first book of stories by Hans Andersen appeared. Although Andersen himself thought the tales were unimportant compared with his novels and plays, they quickly made his name famous. Among the most popular were "The Ugly Duckling" and "The Emperor's New Clothes", although these were still carrying on the old tradition of trying to point a moral as well as entertain.

At much the same time "Struwwelpeter", by Heinrich Hoffman, first appeared in English. This gave dire warnings to all the children who refused to comb their hair or cut their nails and so on! Also "The Water-Babies", by Charles Kingsley, which was published in 1863, contained much the same kind of warnings, with such characters as "Mrs Doasyouwouldbedoneby".

Then in 1869 one of the most famous children's books of all time was published. It was "Alice's Adventures in Wonderland", written by Lewis Carroll and illustrated by John Tenniel. It was not only immensely popular, but also put an end once and for all to the idea that a book for children had to teach something, and if possible point a moral as well.

Nevertheless, there were still many homes in Victorian times where "Alice" could not be read on a Sunday. In fact, the only books usually considered suitable for Sunday reading were either collections of Bible stories, or else books of prayers and hymns. In some families, however, a children's version of "The Pilgrim's Progress", by John Bunyan, was allowed to be read after the children had been to church, or even a story book like "Jessica's First Prayer", by Sarah Smith.

During the years that followed there were far too many children's books to name them all. But a mention must be made of the books by Kate Greenaway, which were among the most delightful produced in the late nine-

38 An illustration by George Cruikshank.

POLLY'S, Peg's, and Poppety's
   Mamma was kind and good;
She gave them each, one happy day,
   A little scarf and hood.

A bonnet for each girl she bought,
   To shield them from the sun;
They wore them in the snow and rain,
   And thought it mighty fun.

But sometimes there were naughty boys,
   Who called to them at play,
And made this rude remark—"My eye!
   Three Grannies out to-day!"

▲
39 An illustration of "Alice through the Looking Glass" by Tenniel.

◄**40** A page from "Under the Window" by Kate Greenaway.

teenth century. Also the books of Rudyard Kipling, particularly the "Just So Stories" and "Rewards and Fairies", have a special place in the history of children's literature, because of their imaginative accounts of long-ago times and far-away places.

A rather interesting point about children's books is that from the first they have always been far more international than the books which have been written for adults. For instance, the stories of Perrault (who was French), the Grimm brothers (German), Hans Andersen (Danish), Mark Twain (American) and Collodi (Italian) are all almost as well-known in England as the books of our own Lewis Carroll and Kipling.

41 Two advertisements for children's books, 1911.

47

8
Newspapers and Magazines

The earliest daily paper was almost certainly "The Daily Courant". It first appeared on 11 March 1702, and consisted of just one sheet, with printing on only one side of the paper. The editor, who was also the printer, was Samuel Buckley, and he said in the first issue that he had "taken care to be furnished with all the news from abroad, in any language". The first edition of the paper had no home news at all. It was entirely filled with foreign news, mostly two or three weeks old, and apparently copied word for word from various papers abroad. Nevertheless, it obviously filled a considerable need, because it soon expanded, first to four pages and then to six, and continued to be published, always under the same editor, until 1735.

As well as "The Daily Courant" there were also various weekly and monthly papers. Many of these were either founded or edited by well-known writers of the time. In 1704, for example, a weekly paper called "The Review" came out, which was edited, as well as almost entirely written, by Daniel Defoe, the author of "Robinson Crusoe". Another magazine, called "The Examiner", was edited by Jonathan Swift, the author of "Gulliver's Travels". Swift was a Tory while Defoe was a Whig, and they often used their magazines to hurl abuse at each other. Then, in 1711, two famous essayists, Richard Steele and Joseph Addison, brought out "The Spectator", which reached the phenomenal circulation (for those days) of 4,000 copies.

Newspapers were soon wielding such power and influence that the government began to be worried. It was not only jealous of the way the papers could sway public opinion, but also so frightened of criticism that it tried to muzzle the press. In 1712 it put a tax of a halfpenny on every paper which was half a sheet or less in size, and a tax of a penny on every paper which consisted of a whole sheet. This was a severe blow, and a number of newspapers and journals ceased publication immediately. But some other newspaper owners thought of a rather clever way of avoiding the tax. As the law only mentioned papers of half a sheet and one sheet, they promptly brought out papers that consisted of two sheets, and which were therefore not liable to pay the new tax.

The newspaper owners also decided to print more advertisements. They thought that if they charged the advertisers for them at so much a line it would give them a considerable new source of revenue. The government at once replied by putting a tax on the advertisements, but by this time people were becoming so determined to have a newspaper that they would buy one whatever the price.

In fact, not only morning papers but even evening papers were soon on sale in London. The first of any importance was called "The Courier", and it made its appearance in 1792, with two separate editions. It even employed

42   The first page of "The Spectator".

The SPECTATOR.

*Non fumum ex fulgore, sed ex fumo dare lucem
Cogitat, ut speciosa dehinc miracula promat.* Hor.

To be Continued every Day.

Thursday, March 1. 1711.

I Have observed, that a Reader seldom peruses a Book with Pleasure 'till he knows whether the Writer of it be a black or a fair Man, of a mild or cholerick Disposition, Married or a Batchelor, with other Particulars of the like nature, that conduce very much to the right Understanding of an Author. To gratify this Curiosity, which is so natural to a Reader, I design this Paper, and my next, as Prefatory Discourses to my following Writings, and shall give some Account in them of the several Persons that are engaged in this Work. As the chief Trouble of Compiling, Digesting and Correcting will fall to my Share, I must do my self the Justice to open the Work with my own History.

I was born to a small Hereditary Estate, which I find, by the Writings of the Family, was bounded by the same Hedges and Ditches in *William* the Conqueror's Time that it is at present, and has been delivered down from Father to Son whole and entire, without the Loss or Acquisition of a single Field or Meadow, during the Space of six hundred Years. There goes a Story in the Family, that when my Mother was gone with Child of me about three Months, she dreamt that she was brought to Bed of a Judge: Whether this might proceed from a Law-Suit which was then depending in the Family, or my Father's being a Justice of the Peace, I cannot determine; for I am not so vain as to think it presaged any Dignity that I should arrive at in my future Life, though that was the Interpretation which the Neighbourhood put upon it. The Gravity of my Behaviour at my very first Appearance in the World, and all the Time that I sucked, seemed to favour my Mother's Dream: For, as she has often told me, I threw away my Rattle before I was two Months old, and would not make use of my Coral 'till they had taken away the Bells from it.

As for the rest of my Infancy, there being nothing in it remarkable, I shall pass it over in Silence. I find, that, during my Nonage, I had the Reputation of a very sullen Youth, but was always a Favourite of my School-Master, who used to say, *that my Parts were solid and would wear well.* I had not been long at the University, before I di-

stinguished my self by a most profound Silence: For during the Space of eight Years, excepting in the publick Exercises of the College, I scarce uttered the Quantity of an hundred Words; and indeed do not remember that I ever spoke three Sentences together in my whole Life. Whilst I was in this Learned Body I applied my self with so much Diligence to my Studies, that there are very few celebrated Books, either in the Learned or the Modern Tongues, which I am not acquainted with.

Upon the Death of my Father I was resolved to travel into Foreign Countries, and therefore left the University, with the Character of an odd unaccountable Fellow, that had a great deal of Learning, if I would but show it. An insatiable Thirst after Knowledge carried me into all the Countries of *Europe*, where there was any thing new or strange to be seen; nay, to such a Degree was my Curiosity raised, that having read the Controversies of some great Men concerning the Antiquities of *Egypt*, I made a Voyage to *Grand Cairo*, on purpose to take the Measure of a Pyramid; and as soon as I had set my self right in that Particular, returned to my Native Country with great Satisfaction.

I have passed my latter Years in this City, where I am frequently seen in most publick Places, tho' there are not above half a dozen of my select Friends that know me; of whom my next Paper shall give a more particular Account. There is no Place of Publick Resort, wherein I do not often make my Appearance; sometimes I am seen thrusting my Head into a Round of Politicians at *Will's*, and listning with great Attention to the Narratives that are made in those little Circular Audiences. Sometimes I smoak a Pipe at *Child's*; and whilst I seem attentive to nothing but the *Post-Man*, over-hear the Conversation of every Table in the Room. I appear on *Sunday* Nights at St. *James's* Coffee-House, and sometimes join the little Committee of Politicks in the Inner-Room, as one who comes there to hear and improve. My Face is likewise very well known at the *Grecian*, the *Cocoa-Tree*, and in the Theaters both of *Drury-Lane*, and the *Hay-Market*. I have been taken for a Merchant upon

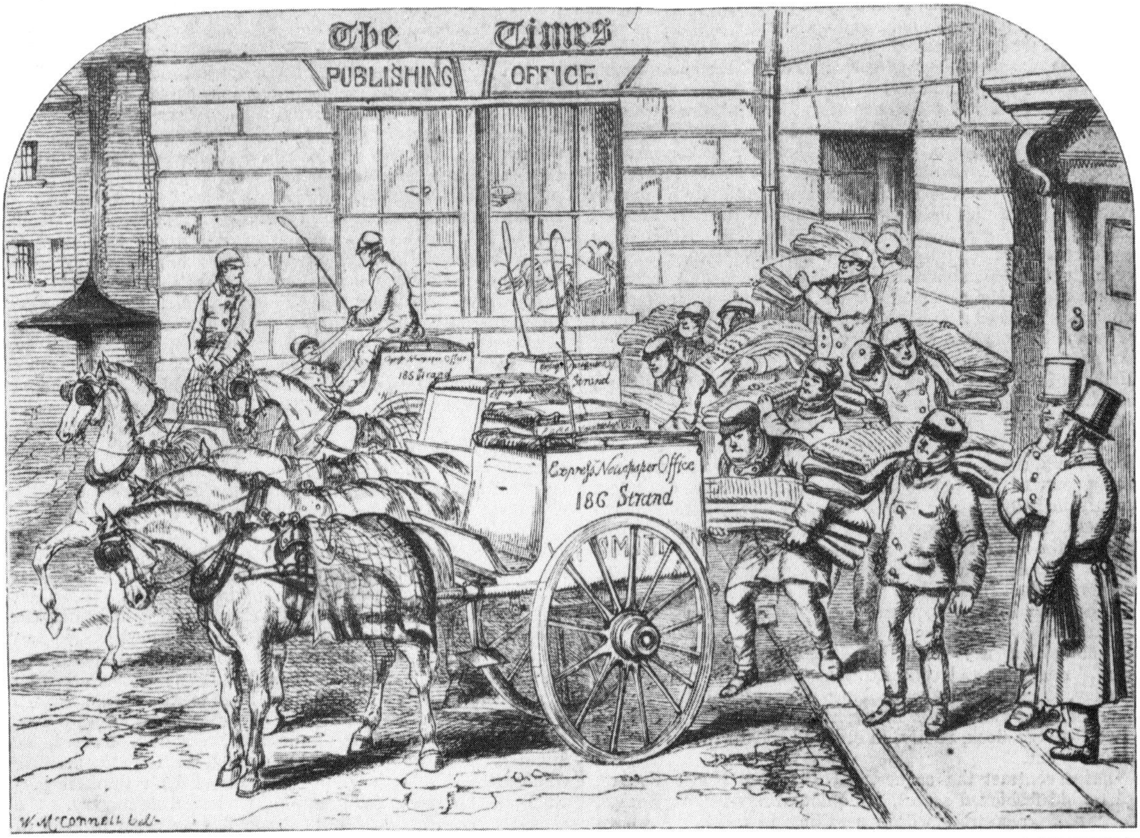
The Times
PUBLISHING OFFICE.
Express Newspaper Office
186 Strand
W. McConnell

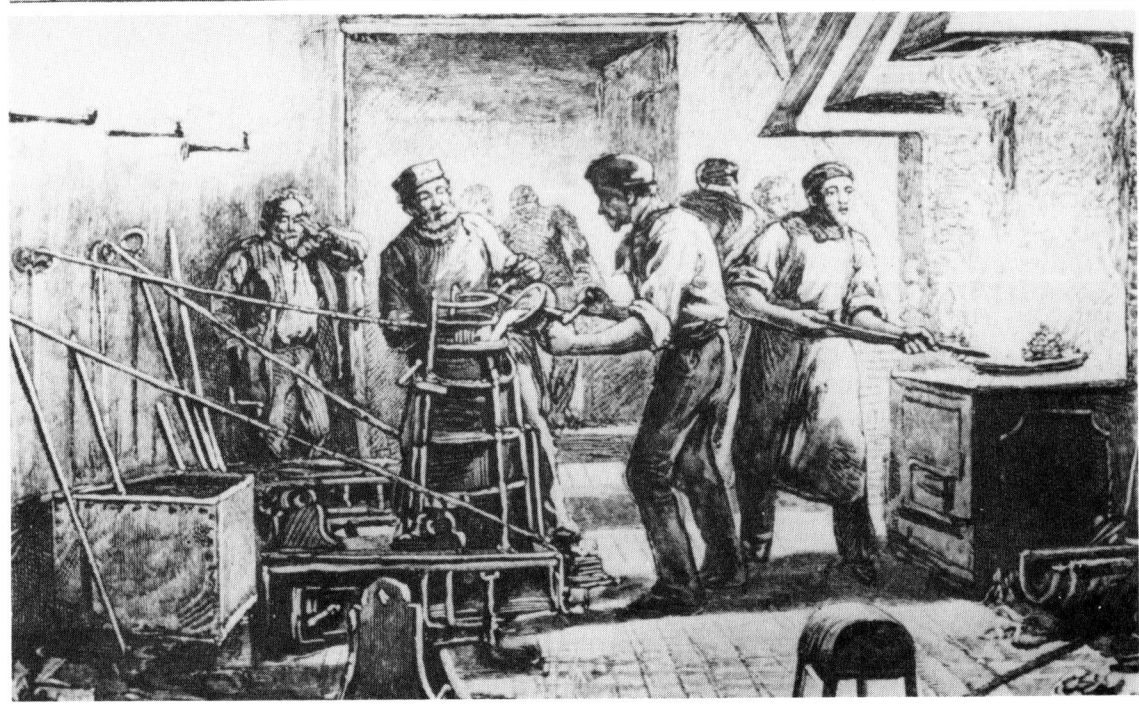

its own newspaper sellers, who used to run through the streets blowing their horns and shouting, between blasts, "News! News! Great news! 'Courier'! Second Edition!"

In 1795 the most famous newspaper of all was founded. The story began when an insurance broker named John Water started looking for a new way to make some extra money. Just by chance he met a man who said he had invented a new and much faster method of printing, and Water decided that it was worth buying the patent. Once Water had set up the press he thought he would use it to print a newspaper. So he started "The Daily Universal Register", and from the first it was an enormous success. Three years later, however, Water decided that the new method of printing was neither as good nor as cheap as he had thought, and so he began printing in the usual, old-fashioned way, and at the same time he changed the name of his paper to "The Times".

From then onwards the history of newspapers is largely the history of "The Times". It was almost certainly "The Times", for instance, that first thought of sending a reporter abroad to send regular reports home. The reporter's name was Henry Crabb Robinson, and although his dispatches seem mainly to have been based on what he had read in the foreign papers rather than on what he had seen for himself, they must have been fascinating to the readers of that period. Similarly, it was probably "The Times" which first sent its own "Special Correspondent" abroad. (By "Special Correspondent" is meant a reporter who is sent to some particular place to cover one specific event.) This was William Howard Russell, and it was his famous report from the Crimea appealing to women to go out and nurse "the sick and suffering soldiers" that inspired Florence Nightingale to set up the first hospital there.

44   The type foundry at "The Times".

In about the middle of the nineteenth century a new name began to appear at the bottom of many newspaper reports. This was the name Reuter, and it belonged to one of the first people to think of setting up a special news service. Paul Julius Reuter had been born at Hesse, in West Germany, but he had begun his news agency in Paris, translating articles, social gossip and other news items, and sending them to papers anywhere which were willing to pay for them. Then Reuter's great opportunity arrived with the coming of the telegraph. As more and more telegraph lines were opened he began to expand his business all over Europe. On the other hand, Reuter's real strength lay in his adaptability and resourcefulness. When there were no telegraph lines available, for instance, he would even make use of carrier pigeons to carry his news items.

In 1860 Reuter moved to London and took out British nationality. From that time onwards his reports became one of the chief sources of news for almost every paper in the country, including "The Times". Today Reuter's is one of the largest suppliers of news in the world, with more than half a million words coming into its central news room every day, and flashed out again within minutes to every corner of the globe.

Local Papers

While the papers in London were expanding, the local papers were also flourishing, although originally they did not give local news but only reprinted the main news which had already appeared in the London press. No one is quite certain which was the first local paper, but "The Worcester News-sheet", started in 1690, was certainly one of the earliest, and rather remarkably it is still being published today, although it is now called "The Worcester Journal". Unfortunately, none of the very early copies of "The Worcester News-sheet" still survive. But there still exists a "Bristol Postboy" of 1704 bear-

TIT-BITS

BOOKS. PERIODICALS. AND NEWSPAPERS IN THE WORLD

No. 2.—Vol. I. [Entered at Stationers' Hall.] PRICE ONE PENNY. [Registered for Transmission Abroad.] Oct. 29, 1881.

TO OUR READERS.

Only a week has elapsed since *Tit-Bits* was sent out into the world to fight its way into the good opinion of the public. Though the time is so short, we are informed that already arrangements are in progress for starting two "imitations" of *Tit-Bits*—one in London, one in the country. Probably in a month or two there will be half-a-dozen imitators.

The conductors of *Tit-Bits* are not dismayed: they expected this, and are prepared for it. They have made arrangements which will, in future, be the means of sending *Tit-Bits* into every town and village in the country. Great expense is being incurred in advertising *Tit-Bits* in London and the provinces, and a successful result is anticipated.

We have received very many letters congratulating us upon No. 1. These have come from far and near, and some of them from gentlemen of position and influence.

We wish to say that we sincerely thank all those who have sent us these letters of encouragement. Our aim will be to produce weekly a pennyworth of interesting reading such as is not to be obtained in any other paper.

During a theatrical engagement in Manchester, Kemble and Lewis were walking one day along the street, when a chimney-sweeper and his boy came up. The boy stared at them with open mouth, and exclaimed, "They be play actors !" "Hold your tongue, you dog !" said the old sweep. "You don't know what you may come to yourself one day."

Motto for a Servants' Hall.— Learn to labour and to wait.

"I thought you told me Mr. Browns fever had gone off," said a gentleman. "So I did," said his companion ; "but I forgot to mention he went off with it."

"Isn't it time you paid me that bill ?" said Stubbs to one of his debtors. "My dear sir," was the consoling reply, "it's not a question of time—it's a question of money."

A London paper once informed its readers that an additional number of sentinels were to be placed in Hyde Park to prevent the robberies of last winter.

A quack doctor on his deathbed willed his property to a lunatic asylum, giving as a reason for doing so that he wished his fortune to go to the liberal class who had patronised him.

A poet was once walking with M. Talleyrand in the street, reciting some of his verses. Talleyrand, perceiving at a distance a man yawning, pointed him out to the poet, saying, "Not so loud—he hears you."

George Colman, getting out of a hackney coach one night, gave the driver a shilling. "This is a bad shilling," said Jarvey. "Then it's all right," said George, with his inimitable chuckle—"yours is a bad coach."

There is a grocer down West who is said to be so mean that he was seen to catch a fly off his counter, hold him up by the hind legs, and look in the cracks of his feet to see if he hadn't been stealing some of his best sugar.

Mr. Jenkins playfully remarked to his wife that in her he possessed four fools. "Who are they ?" she asked. "Beautifool, dutifool, youthfool, and delightfool," said he. "You have the advantage of me, my dear," she replied. "I have but one fool."

A person begging alms of Lord George Gordon, said, "God bless you, my Lord ! you and I have been in all the prisons in London." "What do you mean ?" cried Lord George. "I never was in any prison but the Tower." "That is true, my Lord," said the other, "and I have been in all the rest."

A bad-tempered judge was annoyed by an old gentleman who had a chronic cough, and after repeatedly desiring the crier to keep the court quiet, at length told the offender that he would fine him £100 if he did not cease coughing, when he was met with the reply, "I'll give your lordship £200 if you will stop it for me."

Foote, being once annoyed by a poor fiddler straining harsh discords under his window, sent him a shilling, with a request "that he would play elsewhere, as one scraper at the door was sufficient."

"Why, your hair is getting quite grey," said Mr. Whiffle, the editor, to a friend. "Yes, but there is plenty of it, at least," looking at the editor's head, a Sahara of baldness. "Oh, yes ! mine preferred death to dishonour."

"My dearest Maria," wrote a recently-married husband to his wife. She wrote back, "Dearest,— Let me correct either your grammar or your morals. You address me 'My dearest Maria.' Am I to suppose you have other dear Marias ?"

Dean Ramsay relates that during the long French war two old ladies in Stranraer were going to the kirk, when one said to the other, "Was it no' a wonderful thing that the Breetish were aye victorious over the French in battle ?" "Not a bit," said the other old lady. "Dinna ye ken the Breetish aye say their prayers before gaen into battle ?" The other replied, "But canna the French say their prayers as weel." The reply was most characteristic, "Hoot ! jabbering bodies, who could *understan'* them ?"

Suett, the actor, was very fond of gin, and he had once a landlady with a similar *penchant*. He would order her servant to procure supplies after this fashion : "Betty, go and get a quartern loaf and half a quartern of gin." Off went Betty: she was speedily recalled. "Betty, make it *half* a quartern loaf and a *quartern* of gin." But Betty had not got fairly across the threshold ere the voice was again heard : "Betty, on second thoughts, you may as well make it *all gin !*"

Once on a time an epicurean friend of ours used frequently to dine at the house of a certain gourmet of the county—very wealthy, very fond of good eating, very mean, and selfish. Our friend (a shrewd man) had often noticed that when the ladies left, and the run on the wine became sharper (people drank harder then), the butler came in and whispered to the host, upon which he generally replied, in the most earnest and emphatic way, "Yes, and mind the B.B." This so stirred his curiosity that on one occasion, being on a visit, and meeting the butler out of doors before breakfast, he got him into conversation, and slipped a guinea into his hand. "Davis," he said, "I want you to tell me, between ourselves, just as a matter of curiosity, you know, what your master so often asks for." A phosphorescent smile flitted across the face of David as he looked round at the house, and then coughed twice—"Lord bless you, sir !" he replied. "B.B. ! That's no special vintage, that ain't. Don't you take any of that muck, sir. That's our bottled bottles."

ing the number 91, and a "Norwich Post" of 1708 which is numbered 348. The earliest copy of a local paper which is still being published, though, is a "Stamford Mercury" dated 22 May 1718, which is in the British Museum.

By the middle of the eighteenth century the rivalry among the various local papers had become feverish. Many of them, such as "The Birmingham Gazette" and "The Northampton Mercury" even employed relays of horsemen to rush the latest news from London direct to their offices. But, as time went on, the local papers gave up trying to be first with the national news, because they realized that most of their readers were far more interested in small news items from their own towns or villages.

The most famous local paper of all was "The Manchester Guardian". It was founded in May 1821, by a Quaker, with £1,000 which he had managed to borrow from some friends. It had four pages and cost 7d (including tax), and like all the other local papers of the time it copied its foreign news from the London papers, although it also printed its own local news. At first "The Manchester Guardian" hardly made enough money to keep going. In fact, its first reporter had to take shorthand notes at the local events, rush back to the office, set up the type and even turn the handle of the press himself. Before long, however, the paper became so popular that it began appearing twice a week, and eventually as "The Guardian" became one of the country's greatest daily papers, printed in both Manchester and London.

Magazines

As more and more people learnt to read, a demand developed for light, amusing reading. As a result, George Newnes brought out the weekly magazine, "Tit-Bits", in 1881. It had no long columns of printing or heavy political articles, but just sixteen pages of short, entertaining paragraphs, and within a few months more than a million copies were being sold every week. A similar magazine which first appeared at much the same time was called "Answers to Correspondents" (later shortened to "Answers"). It was begun by an enterprising young man of twenty-two named Alfred Harmsworth. It cost one penny for twelve pages, and had such articles as "Do Women Live Longer than Men?" Later it also became known for its amusing competitions, such as trying to guess the amount of money in the Bank of England on one particular day.

Rather surprisingly, it was a considerable time before any children's papers or magazines appeared. Then, in 1879, "The Boy's Own Paper" was published, quickly followed by "The Girl's Own Paper". Later there was also "The Children's Newspaper", which was founded by a man named Arthur Mee in 1919, and which tried to interest young people in everything that was going on in the world. A little earlier the first "comics" had appeared in the newsagents. (The word "comic" came from America, and was used to describe any cheap children's paper which was filled with cartoons.) Some of these comics, such as "Tiny Tots" and "The Rainbow", were delightful, but by and large they were badly written and badly printed, and merely provided the children with an effortless way of passing the time.

45   "Tit-Bits".   46   overleaf: "The Boy's Own Paper".

THE BOY'S OWN PAPER

No. 559.—Vol. XI.   SATURDAY, SEPTEMBER 28, 1889.   Price One Penny.
[ALL RIGHTS RESERVED.]

Hunting with Cheetah.

A MIDDY AMONGST THE SLAVERS.

By Arthur Lee Knight,

Author of "Basil Woolecombe, Midshipman," "The Adventures of a Midshipmite," etc., etc.

PART II.

THE boat duty in connection with the suppression of the slave-traffic is very trying and dangerous work for our "boys in blue." The boats are sometimes sent away from the ship on a separate cruise for perhaps a week or a fortnight at a

9
Books for Everyone

New Methods

When printing was first invented it was a slow, tedious business. Every single operation, from arranging the type to applying the ink, had to be done separately by hand. Nevertheless, it was well over three hundred years after the death of Caxton before any really significant advance was made in the methods of printing.

The breakthrough finally came in 1814. Instead of using the old-fashioned hand-presses, the owners of "The Times" decided to install a press worked by steam. The type still had to be arranged by hand, but even so the new press was an enormous success, because it could print no fewer than fifteen hundred copies of the paper in an hour.

In the late nineteenth century printing finally became fully mechanized. Two famous printing machines, called the Mono-type and the Linotype, were introduced at about the same time. Instead of the printer having to arrange the letters in order, he now merely used a keyboard that looked something like a typewriter, and the machine cast the letters out of hot liquid metal as they were required.

Since then there have been all kinds of innovations in the way books and papers are printed. Unfortunately, they have not all been very popular with the printers them-selves. There have, indeed, even been strikes because printers have been afraid that new, improved methods of printing might mean that fewer printers would be needed to work the machines.

As well as new methods of printing, there have been many attempts to find new ways of making paper. Long before Caxton's time people had discovered that the best way of making paper was by using old rags. Oddly enough, however, the paper was always imported, usually from Italy or Spain, and it was not until early in the sixteenth century that the first paper mill in this country was opened in Hertfordshire, by a man named John Tate.

As the demand for paper increased, people also tried various other ways of producing it. Straw was used first, in the early nineteenth century, but it was not found to be very satisfactory. Then wood was tried, and this proved excellent for making newspapers and cheap magazines, which were read and then thrown away, but no good for books which were meant to last, because the paper soon became yellow and brittle.

The first paper-making machine was invented in France at the very end of the eighteenth century and within a few years the machines were in use in England as well. Today paper-making machines produce enormous ribbons of paper, out of either rags or wood, which are several metres wide and

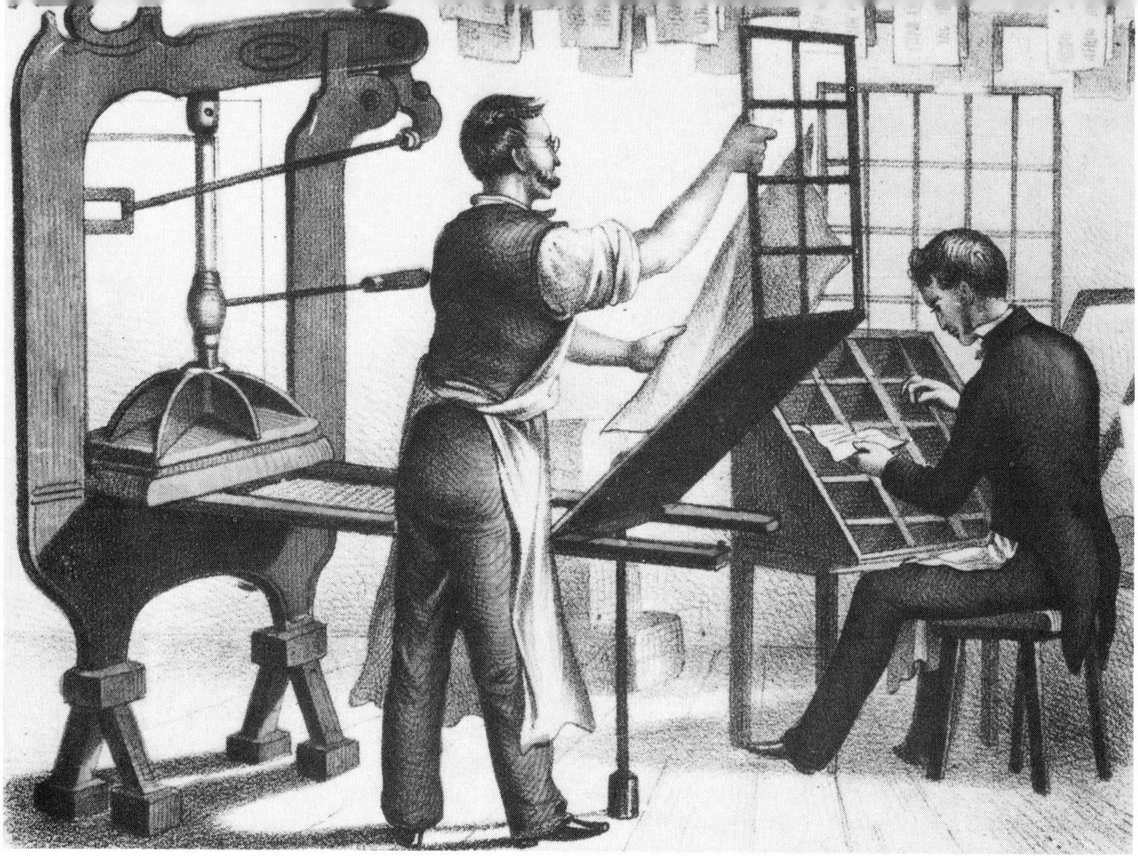

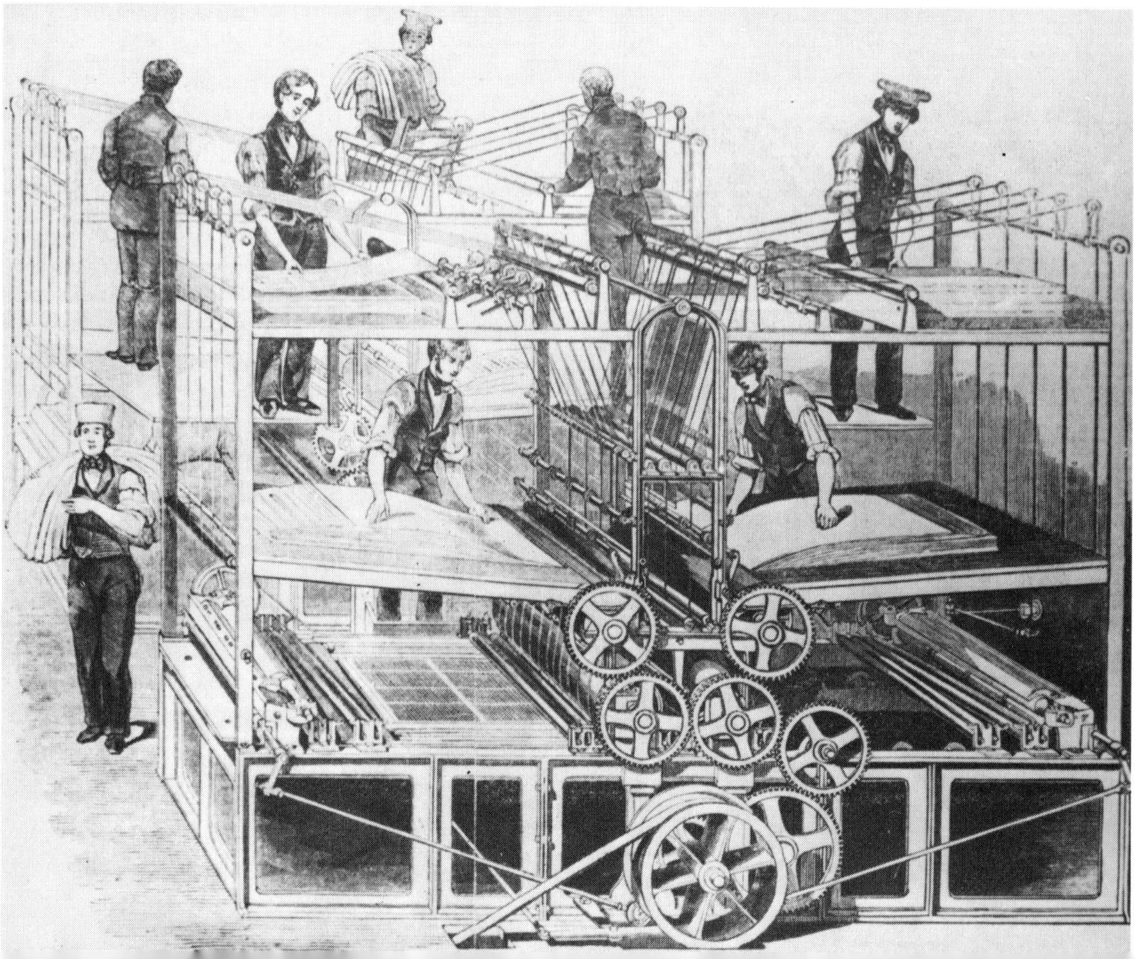

as much as three kilometres long. These are later cut up into smaller pieces.

People knew how to print pictures long before they could print writing, but it was a

◀47   A nineteenth-century hand printing press.

slow, time-consuming process to make the blocks they needed, because these all had to be cut or engraved by hand. Then, early in the nineteenth century, photography was invented, and it was not long before an entirely new method of producing book illustrations was discovered. A photograph of the drawing that was to be reproduced was printed on a specially prepared zinc plate. Then the plate was put into a bath of acid, which ate away the parts of the plate which were not to be printed. This meant that the picture stood out in relief, and after the zinc plate had been mounted on a piece of wood it could be used for printing in the usual way.

This method of printing pictures from "line-blocks" is still in use today. It is sometimes even used for printing coloured illustrations, but in that case a separate block has to

◀48   The steam-powered printing machine used by "The Illustrated London News", 1843.

▲
50   Book binders' factory of the nineteenth century.

51 A choice of leather bindings.

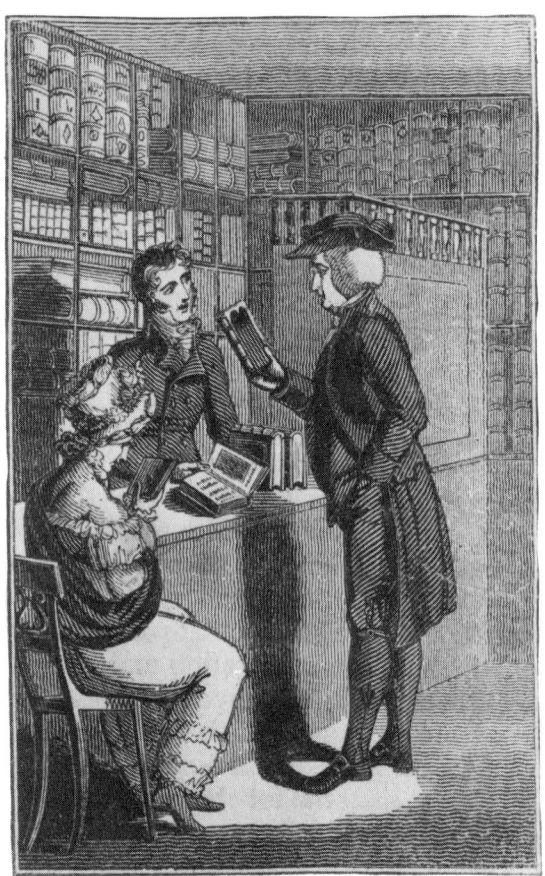

52 The Bookseller, 1820s.

be made for each colour required. Nowadays there are various other ways of producing illustrations too, and the one the publisher chooses depends largely on the time and the amount of money he has to spare, which depends mainly, of course, on the amount he is going to charge for the book.

Until the end of the eighteenth century a publisher usually sent his books unbound to the bookseller. Then the person who bought one of the books would tell the bookseller what kind of binding he wanted. The bookseller would send the book away to a binder, who would bind the book in fine leather, and usually add the title and perhaps some decoration in beautiful gold tooling, as it was called. By about 1820, however, books were arriving

at the booksellers already bound. What was more, by this time they were more often bound in cloth than in leather. A few years later machines were invented to make the cloth bindings, and also to attach them to the rest of the book by a process called "casing".

Not long after cased books became commonplace some books were given paper wrappers, or "dust jackets". But it was not until about 1890 that "dust-jackets" became usual on nearly all books. They then became not only a protection for the books, but also an eye-catching advertisement, as they were printed with bright designs on the front, and information about the book on the back and on the flaps.

Paper-backs

There had, of course, been cheap paper-back books, sold by chapmen since the seventeenth century. But these had been poorly written, poorly printed books, little better than very badly produced comics. There were no cheap copies of the classics until almost the end of the nineteenth century, when some go-ahead publishers, like Dent, began printing books by such writers as Shakespeare and Dickens in such large numbers that they could sell them for as little as a shilling a copy.

It was still some time before anyone thought of producing paper-back reprints of well-known books, though. Then in 1935 Sir Allen Lane published the first of the famous "Penguin Books", as he decided to call them. The book was "Ariel", a life of the poet Shelley, by André Maurois, and it cost the amazingly low price (even for those days) of 6d.

Since then millions of paper-back books have been sold every year. In fact, in the case of every type of literature (except books for schools and colleges) many times more paper-back books than hard-back books are sold. Even some public libraries are now buying paper-backs, particularly in the case of fiction books, and putting transparent wrappers or "sleeves" on them, instead of spending money on hard-back books.

53   Penguins on sale at Waterloo, 1946, to celebrate the 90th birthday of George Bernard Shaw.

New Tastes

Not only the format of books, but also their length has changed considerably over the years. In Victorian times some popular books stretched to two or sometimes even three volumes. Even books by such famous writers as Charles Dickens or Thomas Hardy nearly always contained five or six hundred pages of very small print. Today, on the other hand, people generally prefer much shorter stories. With so many other forms of entertainment available, such as radio and television, most people do not want to spend days, or even weeks, reading a book. The novels of Grahame Greene, for example, who is generally regarded as one of the finest writers of this century, are rarely more than about three hundred pages long.

Another interesting development in comparatively recent times has been the increase in the number of women writers. Until the middle of the eighteenth century, or even later, women rarely, if ever, attempted to write books, either fiction or non-fiction. This is not altogether surprising, because even when girls began to receive a similar kind of education to their brothers they were hardly ever encouraged to make use of their talents. Among the first popular women writers were the Brontë sisters, who lived in the early nineteenth century. But even they originally thought that they ought to assume men's names (they called themselves Currer, Ellis and Acton Bell) in order to get their books published. Then, as time went on, more and more women writers became established, although even today there are not nearly as many front-rank women writers as men in most branches of literature.

Publishing Today

Today well over twenty-five thousand new books are published in our country every year. They vary from books of nursery rhymes to books for students and teachers

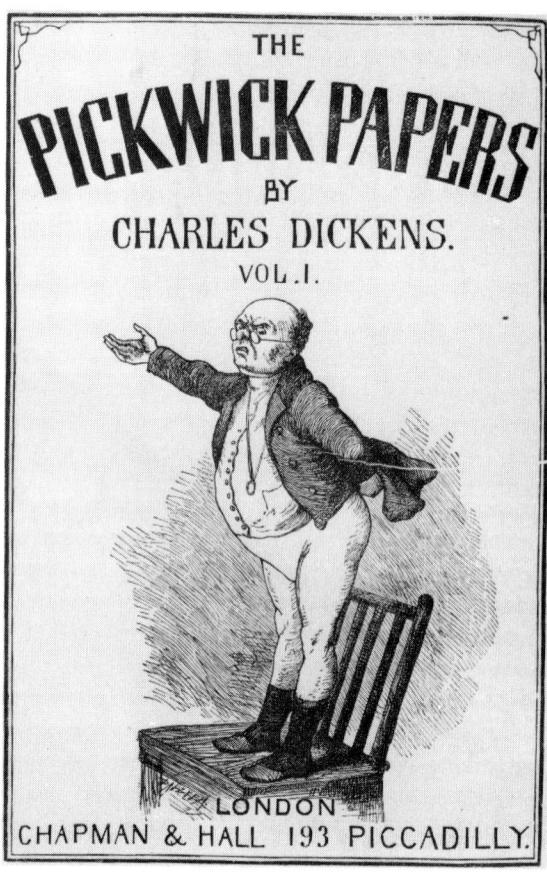

54   The title page of "The Pickwick Papers". Books were much longer than nowadays.

written by university professors. Basically, however, they are all produced in much the same way, and all involve a considerable number of different people in their planning and production.

First, of course, there is the author, or perhaps a group of authors. Then there is sometimes an illustrator, who may be either an artist or perhaps a photographer. Next comes the publisher, who decides which books he thinks he can sell, and provides all the money that is needed to publish and promote the book. Then comes the printer, who as well as printing the book normally provides the cover. He is usually also required to provide the dust-jacket, if the book has a hard cover. Then, last of all, there is the bookseller, except in the case of school books, which are usually sold direct to the schools by the publishers' representatives.

One interesting point is that the publisher's name must appear by law on the first page of every book. Also by law the printer's name must appear somewhere, either at the front or at the back of the book. In the case of living authors there is usually also the letter C in a circle, followed by the author's name at the front of the book, which means that the copyright of the book belongs to the author, and that, by law, no one is allowed to copy it without the author's permission.

10
Libraries

There must have been libraries for almost as long as there have been books. But in this country, at least, they nearly all belonged privately to some rich or important nobleman until the end of the Middle Ages. Then at the beginning of the fifteenth century a certain Duke Humphrey, who was the fourth son of Henry IV, gave a collection of handwritten books to Oxford University for the use of the students.

The University was so pleased with the books that it built a special room to house them. Then it furnished its new library with rows of presses (an old word for shelves), desks and benches. "We wish you could see the students," wrote one of the university scribes to Duke Humphrey, "bending over the books you have given us in their thirst and greediness for knowledge."

Little more than a hundred years later, however, England became a Protestant country. As a result, nearly all the books in Duke Humphrey's library were condemned as being "Popish" or Catholic. This meant not only that all the books were destroyed, except for a mere four or five, but that even the shelves and all the furniture were burnt.

Towards the end of the sixteenth century a scholar named Sir Thomas Bodley became interested in the library. He rebuilt the roof and fitted new presses, desks and benches. Then, having travelled all over Europe in the search for books, he finally opened the Bodleian Library, as it was called, in November 1602.

There was another early library at Cambridge University. No one knows exactly when it was founded, but it is certain that by 1425 it had fifty-two books. We also know that the books were originally chained up (just as they were at Oxford), and that it was not decided to unchain them until 1626.

55　The Bodleian Library, Oxford.

It was some years before London had a library to compare with those at Oxford and Cambridge. Then in 1759 the British Museum was opened, in a building known as Montague House. Right from the beginning the museum had an enormous collection of books on almost every subject, mostly presents from people who were interested in helping to found a new library, including a large number given by the King, George II.

The library, with the rest of the British Museum, moved to its present building in Russell Square, in the centre of London, in the mid-nineteenth century, and it now houses well over two million books. Even the catalogue fills more than fourteen hundred volumes, as every book in the library is carefully listed on a separate, small piece of paper, which is then pasted in its appropriate place. In fact, the task of adding new books to the catalogue is never-ending, as a copy of every new book published in Britain has to be sent to the British Museum by law. The other libraries that also have the right to a copy of every new book are the Bodleian and the Cambridge University Library, the national libraries of Scotland and Wales and the library of Trinity College, in Dublin.

All the early libraries were designed purely for the use of scholars. But as more and more people learnt how to read, a demand grew for libraries which were open to everyone. As a result, quite a number of churches began to make small collections of books, and as early as the beginning of the seventeenth century a few enterprising towns, such as Norwich and Coventry, actually opened the first public reading rooms.

It was nearly a hundred years before the first "circulating libraries" were opened, however. (The word "circulating" means that

56   The reading room of the British Museum, 1842.

▲
57 Part of the gallery of the circular Reading Room of the British Library.

58 Hall's Library at Margate, 1789 – a circulating library portrayed by Thomas Malton as a social meeting place.

books could be taken away in return for a small payment, and read at home.) No one knows who was the first person to have the idea of allowing the books to be taken away, nor where the first circulating library was opened, but most people think that it was probably in Scotland. One of the earliest was certainly in a corner of a bookshop in Edinburgh. It was opened by a man named Allan Ramsey, who was also quite well-known as a poet. Among the people who often went to the bookshop was Sir Walter Scott (the author of "Ivanhoe"), although whether he actually ever made use of the circulating library himself is not known.

By the end of the eighteenth century there was a circulating library in practically every town in the country. But the libraries still only reached a comparatively small section of the population. In rural areas, where most of the people lived, there were still no libraries (and rarely any bookshops either), and in any case the vast majority of the country people were still illiterate at that time.

Then in 1832 Parliament made a grant so that more schools could be built, and this meant that an ever-increasing number of people learnt to read, and wanted to be able to borrow books. Nothing was done about the matter, however, until 1850, when, against considerable opposition, an Act was passed which allowed boroughs to collect a half-penny in the pound rate in order to build libraries (although not to buy books!). As a result, Norwich immediately voted the money to build the country's first public library, although, in fact, it was in Manchester that the first library was actually opened, in September 1852. A few years later, when the amount that could be collected was increased to a penny in the pound, and it could be used to buy books as well as to erect buildings, public

59   The Manchester Free Library, 1852.

60 With the spread of literacy in the mid-nineteenth century, cotton workers came to read the news at the Camp-field Library, Manchester, 1862.

libraries began to be opened in nearly all the big cities.

There were still no libraries in the smaller towns or villages, however, despite the fact that more and more people were learning to read at this time because of the rapid spread of education. Then in 1870 a law was passed which made it compulsory for all children to attend school, and the demand for libraries soon became a matter of urgency.

The difficulty was that the majority of towns had no money to spare for building libraries. It usually took all their meagre resources just to provide such necessities as houses and hospitals. But then, as if in answer to a prayer, a very rich and very generous man named Andrew Carnegie came to their rescue.

Andrew Carnegie had been born in Scotland, but while he was still a boy his family had moved to Pittsburgh, in the United States of America. There, with various other poor boys, he had been befriended by a wealthy man who had allowed him to use his library, and Carnegie had vowed that, if he himself ever became rich, he would build free lending libraries in Britain. Carnegie did become rich. Indeed, he became a millionaire many times over. He also remembered his promise to provide free libraries for the people in the country where he had been born. As a result, "Carnegie libraries", as they came to be called, were soon being opened all over Britain, due entirely to the generosity of this one remarkable man.

The next step forward was the provision of children's libraries. At first, children had not even been allowed to enter a public library until they reached the age of fourteen. Then in 1882 the first children's library was opened, at Nottingham, with its own staff and its own catalogue, owing to a gift of £500 from a Member of Parliament named Samuel Morley. Some other towns later decided to follow suit and provide libraries for children, but it was not until 1919, when an Act was passed that allowed local councils to spend money on children's books, that the situation really changed. Then the more progressive councils began providing separate rooms for children in their libraries, with special small tables and chairs, and special librarians who were particularly interested in the needs of young readers.

Naturally the early libraries were very different from the libraries we have today. For one thing, people were not allowed to browse and then decide what they wanted to borrow. Even as late as 1894 people had to know which book they wanted, and then go up to a counter and ask the librarian to find it for them. Also there were no reading rooms in the early libraries where people could read newspapers and magazines. Indeed, even when these were provided they were usually very uncomfortable places, with no seats and the papers fixed to tall reading desks. What was more, even as late as the Second World War there were large notices saying "Silence" on the walls in all the libraries, and there was none of the quiet, happy hubbub that we are used to in our libraries nowadays.

Today every town in the country has its own library. It is usually a bright, cheerful place, where there are all kinds of activities, from "Story-times" for small children to art exhibitions. The librarians are different too, and no longer merely hand over the books. An ever-increasing number of them now have

61   A public library, 1950s.

a degree in librarianship, and can give the readers expert advice on the books. The greatest change of all in recent years, though, has been in the books themselves. These now range from large, attractive picture books for toddlers to books in specially large print for people whose eyesight is poor. How surprised the monks of long ago, who spent their lives copying out books, would be if they could know how many people have the chance to read and enjoy books today, and surely how pleased they would be as well.

Date List

c. 5000 BC	The Egyptians learn to write.
c. 700 BC	Our present-day alphabet invented by the Romans.
105 AD	Paper invented in China.
Early 2nd century	The first codices produced.
4th century	Parchment replaces papyrus.
c. 698	Lindisfarne Gospels written.
1087	The Domesday Book compiled.
1270	Paper making spreads to Europe.
1444	Gutenberg begins printing at Strasburg.
1477	Caxton's first book printed.
1516	Tyndale begins translating the New Testament into English.
1602	The Bodleian Library opened at Oxford.
1611	The Authorised Version of the Bible published.
1623	Shakespeare's complete works first printed.
1650	First story books for children.
1702	First daily newspaper appears.
1820	First bound books appear.
1852	First Public Library opened (at Manchester).
1882	First children's library opened (at Nottingham).
1890	Books appear with dust-jackets.
1935	Sir Allen Lane publishes the first "Penguin Books".

Books for Further Reading

Susan Bartlett,
Books,
Chatto, Oliver and Boyd

Sean Jennett,
The Making of Books,
Faber and Faber, 1974

Alison Leach,
Books,
Franklyn Watts, 1977

Francis Meynell,
English Printed Books,
Collins

George D. Painter,
William Caxton,
Chatto and Windus, 1976

Alan G. Thomas,
Great Books and Book Collectors
Weidenfeld and Nicolson, 1975

Helen Wodzicka,
The Printer and his Craft,
Wayland, 1972

Index

The numbers in **bold type** refer to the figure numbers of the illustrations

advertisements 40; **24, 41**
Aesop's Fables 41
Alfred the Great 14
"Alice through the Looking
    Glass" 45; **39**
Andersen, Hans 45, 47
Anglo-Saxon Chronicle 15
"Answers" 53
Apocalypse 19
Ascham, Roger 41
Assyrians 6
Atticus, Titus 7
Authorised Version of the Bible
    33

Bede, Venerable 12, 15; **8**
Benedictional of St Aethelwold
    15; **11**
Beowulf 14
bestiary 20
Bible 8, 14, 16, 20, 24, 33
bindings 30, 58
Bodleian Library 15, 62–63; **55**
bookbinders 36; **50**
booklets **37**
"Book of Courtesy" 27
Book of Hours 17
bookseller **52**
"Boy's Own Paper" 53; **46**
British Museum 12, 14–15,
    17, 63; **56**

Caedmon 12
"Canterbury Tales" 21, 27; **23**
Carnegie, Andrew 66
Carroll, Lewis 45–46
Caxton, William 24, 27, 30–31,
    36, 38, 55; **24**
censorship 31, 33–34
chained bibles 33; **28**
chapbooks 41–42; **35, 36**

Chaucer, Geoffrey 20, 37; **23**
"Children's Newspaper" 53
Chinese printers **18**
Cicero 7
circulating libraries 63, 65
clay tablets **2**
Codex Sinaiticus 8
colophons 31; **25**
comics 53
Constantine, Emperor 8
copperplate engravings 40
Coryat, Thomas 31
Coverdale, Miles 33
craft guilds 31
Cruikshank, George 45; **38**
cuneiform writing 6; **2**

"Daily Courant" 48
Dead Sea Scrolls 4
Defoe, Daniel 48
Domesday Book 16
Drake, Sir Francis 38
Dürer, Albrecht 40; **32**

Egyptians 6, 8
Erasmus 33

Fleet Street 31
Fust, Johann 24

Geoffrey of Monmouth 20
"Golden Legend" 17, 24
Greeks 7
Greenaway, Kate 45; **40**
Grimm Brothers 45, 47
Guild of Stationers 31, 33
Gutenberg, Johann 24, 30; **19**

Halls Library 58
hand printing press 47
Henry VIII, King 32–33

hieroglyphics 6; **1**
Holbein, Hans 40; **33**
Holinshed, Raphael 37

illumination 11; **12, 14, 15**
illustrations 8, 11, 17, 38, 40,
    45, 57–58, 60

Janeway, James 41

Kells, Book of 14; **10**
King Arthur 27, 41
Kingsley, Charles 45
Kipling, Rudyard 47

Langland, William 21, 37
Lear, Edward 45
leather bindings **51**
libraries 10, 19, 62, 64–67;
    60, 61
Lindisfarne Gospels 12; **6, 7**
linotype machine 55; **49**
Luttrell Psalter 17; **13**

Manchester Free Library 59
"Manchester Guardian" 53
Manutius, Aldus 31
missals 16–17
Moabite Stone 7
monks 10–11, 16–17, 19; **5**
moral education **34**
movable type 24; **20**

Newbery, John 42
newspapers 35, 40, 48, 51, 53
"Nuremberg Chronicle" 40

Oxford University 62

paper 22–23
paper-back books 59

paper-making 22, 55; **17**
papyrus 6–8
parchment 8
Penguin Books 59; **53**
Pergamon, King of 8
Phoenicians 6
"Pickwick Papers" 54
"Pilgrim's Progress" 45
Plantin, Christopher 31
printed books 22
printer's workshop 26
printing 23–24, 60
psalters 16–17, 24; **21**
publishers 36, 60

Raleigh, Sir Walter 38
Rameses II 6
Reuter, Paul Julius 51

Schoeffer, Peter 24, 33
scribes 19; **3**
scriptorium 10, 16
Shakespeare, William 37, 59; **30**
Sherborne Abbey 17
Siferwas, John 17
"Spectator" 48; **42**
"Stamford Mercury" 53
Stationers' Company 36
steam-powered printing machine 48
Stow, John 36
Swift, Jonathan 48

tax on newspapers 48
"Times" 51, 55; **43, 44**
"Tit-Bits" 53; **45**

"True Encounter" 35
Tyndale, William 33; **27**

vellum 8
"Vision of Piers Plowman" 21
Voragine, de 17

Water, John 51
Whas, John 17
Wolfe, John 35
woodcuts 39–42, 45
"Worcester News-sheet" 51
writing 5
Wyclif, John 20; **16**
Wynkyn de Worde 31